Year 6 Contents

To the student

We use language to express our thoughts, feelings, opinions and experiences; and to communicate with others. We might write stories, emails, diaries, greetings, lists, poems, reports, personal recounts and much more.

Language is constantly evolving as human knowledge grows and lifestyles change. New words enter the language while others die out when no longer useful. Thousands of words in use today have their roots in the ancient languages of Latin and Greek. For example, *mobile phone* — two words with a modern spin on the Latin 'root' *moveo motus* (I move) and the Greek 'root' *phone* (a sound).

When we write, we need to construct sentences that make sense and sound right, and spell our words correctly, so that others can understand what we mean.

This book will help you become 'spelling wise' and 'writing ready'. Spelling is very closely linked to grammar (the way we put our sentences together).

In this book, you will learn how words look and sound, and how to use these words correctly in your writing. When we write, we are constantly adding **endings** to words, so that what we write sounds right and makes sense.

Common endings: -s, -es, -ing, -ed, -y, -er, -est and -ly

You will also learn how **prefixes** change the meanings of words and how **suffixes** show grammatical function.

Prefixes: dis- (*like*, ***dis**like*), en- (*close*, ***en**close*), re- (*turn*, ***re**turn*)

Suffixes: -able (as in the adjective *like**able***), -ment (as in the noun *amaze**ment***) and -en (as in the verb *straight**en***)

This book contains tips and spelling rules to help you become a proficient speller. Check out the **Top 3 Spelling Rules** on the back page!

Good spellers know how to see, say and spell many words. They remember what words LOOK like. They also know how to change words in their writing so that their texts sound right and make sense.

About the author

Del has enjoyed a long career in education as a specialist teacher (Learning Difficulties), education adviser and regional coordinator (English). She has written extensively for parents, teachers and students, and is a well-known and respected author nationally and internationally. Her publications cover a diverse range of print and electronic materials in English grammar, spelling, reading, writing and comprehension. She is the author of the popular *Reading Quest* books, a series of readers written for the older, reluctant reader.

Among her latest works are *Blake's Guide to Comprehension*, *Blake's Grammar Guide for primary students* and *Targeting Grammar*.

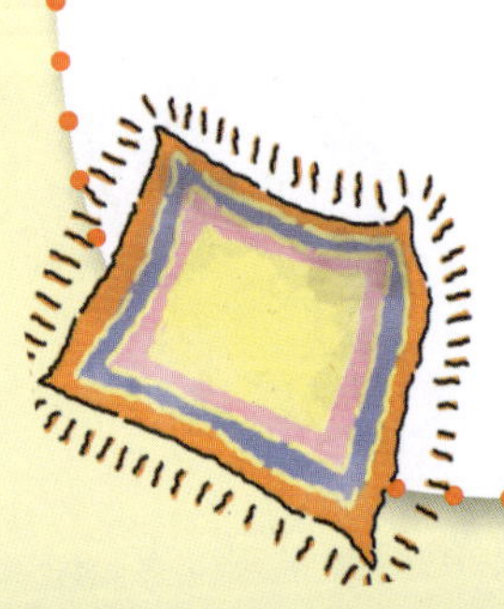

How to Use This Book

Your *Targeting Spelling Activity Book* is set out in units. Each unit contains the following activities. There is a review at the end of each term (eight units of work), so you can check your progress.

SEE & SAY

incur
indicate
individual

SEE & SAY

This is a list of words that provides a focus for each unit. The words in this list target a particular spelling skill and are written in patterns to help you with your learning. Look at these words and say them aloud several times. Say the ends of the words clearly to help you to remember the whole word.

In multi-syllable words, the emphasis is usually on the first syllable, and we tend to 'slur' over the middle or the end of the word. This slurring is called the *schwa* sound (*uh*) and is very common in English. Slurring over syllables without a clear picture of what they look like is one of the main reasons that words are spelt incorrectly.

The See & Say words are a 'warm-up' for the activities that follow.

Not only will you learn how to spell and use these words, you will have opportunities to build a vocabulary that will enhance your own writing.

WORD EXTRA

impossible inaccurate

WORD EXTRA

Two words have been included for revision. They are used frequently in writing and are often misspelt. Space is provided for you to add two or three other words that you find troublesome.

TIPS FOR MEMORISING SPELLING

Remember, **prefixes** and **suffixes** are constant in their spelling.

1. Write the word in large letters. Highlight the syllables in different colours. Close your eyes. Say the word and picture each syllable. Open your eyes and write the word *from memory*.
2. Count the number of syllables (beats) in a word. Draw a box for each syllable. Write a syllable in each box. Run your finger under the boxes as you say the word three times, focusing on what the syllables *look* like.

   Write the word *from memory*. Make sure you connect the syllables (**volcano** not **vol ca no**).

MEMORY TRAINING

Spelling is a skill that requires you to remember the words you want to write. When you see this sign, go back to a previous *See and Say* list and say the words two or three times, focusing on what they look and sound like. Then write as many words as you can remember. Soon, they will start to roll off the end of your pencil!

The more you write, the better your spelling will be.

Prefixes: in-, im-

Many English words have their roots in the ancient language of Latin. Knowing the origins of words helps us to understand both meaning and spelling. The **prefixes** in- and im- mean 'in', 'into' or 'upon'. In Latin, ***pono*** *(positus) = I place, so **impose** = to place upon;* ***halo*** *= I breathe, so **inhale** = to breathe in.* The **prefixes** in- and im- also mean 'not' and are often used to write **antonyms**. *Examples: **in**sane, **in**accurate, **im**polite, **im**possible*

SEE & SAY

incur	inferior	inhabit	implore	impatient	immaculate
indicate	inflict	indulge	impulse	impose	immense
individual	inhale	invade	impress	imitate	immunise

1 Choose a word from the *See and Say* list to complete these sentences.

Parents are asked to ____________________ their children against a range of diseases.

The government could ____________________ higher taxes on luxury imported cars.

Dad is careful not to ____________________ petrol fumes when he is filling the car.

Koalas ____________________ eucalypt woodlands and forests.

Kai looked ____________________, from his sleek hair to the tips of his polished boots.

REVIEW

Verb Tense: When we write, we use **verbs** to show when things are happening.

1 **Present time (tense)** Add -s or -es when the subject is 'he', 'she' or 'it'. *(He jumps.)*
Add -ing to show continuous action. *(He is jump**ing**.)*

2 **Past time (tense)** Add -ed to regular verbs. *(He jump**ed**.)*
Add -ing to show continuous action. *(He was jump**ing**.)*

3 **Future time (tense)** Insert will before the verb. *(He **will jump**.)*

Check out the rules for Common Endings on the back page.

2 Complete this table of verbs.

	Add -s or -es	Add -ing	Add -ed
indicate			
imitate			
inhale			
immunise			
indulge			
impress			

3 Add the prefixes to the base word to build other words. Check any meanings.

im / de / com / ex → **press**

____
____
____
____

im / de / com / ex → **pose**

____
____
____
____

TARGETING SPELLING 6 © PASCAL PRESS ISBN 9781925490244

WORD EXTRA impossible inaccurate

Synonyms are words that are similar in meaning.
Examples: flower, blossom; odd, strange; pretty, attractive, beautiful

4 **Colour the pairs of words that are synonyms. Use a different colour for each pair.**

imitate	implore	immense	indicate	immerse	inferior	indulge
point	shoddy	pamper	beg	copy	huge	dip

TIP

When a **multi-syllable verb** ends in **-ade**, **-ide**, **-ode** or **-ude**, change the **de** to **s** before adding **-ion**. *Examples: decide, decision; erode, erosion; conclude, conclusion*
Some **verbs** require an **extra syllable** before adding **-tion**, so that the noun can be pronounced more easily.
Examples: import, import•tion, importātion; explore, explor•tion, explorātion; prepare, prepar•tion, preparātion; expose, expos•tion, exposition

5 **Using the tip above, change these verbs to nouns by adding -ion.**

invade ____________________ implode ____________________
immunise ____________________ impose ____________________
inhale ____________________ imitate ____________________
indicate ____________________ implement ____________________

6 **Write antonyms using the prefixes in-, im- or un-.**

____possible ____correct ____sure ____sane
____fertile ____defeated ____probable ____likely
____polite ____important ____famous ____active

7 **Match each adjective to its meaning by writing its number in the box. Use a dictionary to help you.**

1 impulsive 2 imposing 3 inhabitable 4 impressive
5 indulgent 6 inferior 7 invasive 8 imminent

☐	about to happen; approaching; near	☐	suitable to live in
☐	grand; striking; eye-catching	☐	lower in rank/quality; second-class
☐	intruding on someone/something	☐	acting rashly without forethought
☐	being over-generous; soft-hearted	☐	causing admiration for quality or skill

Prefixes: dis-

The **prefix** dis- shows something lacking or opposing. It means 'not', 'away' or 'apart'. *Examples: obey, **dis**obey; honour, **dis**honour; ease, **dis**ease*
In Latin, *pono positus = I place or put, so **dispose** = to put away.*

SEE & SAY

disease	discredit	disembark	disgust	dispense	dismiss
disaster	discharge	disfigure	dispose	disperse	dislocate
discuss	discount	disguise	dispatch	dispute	dissolve

1 Add endings to the words in bold to complete the sentences.

dislocate Ty fell heavily from his horse, ____________________ his shoulder.

discount Prices at the local supermarket are regularly ____________________.

disease Scientists continually work on cures for infectious ____________________.

discharge Smoke billows from chimneys, ____________________ pollutants into the air.

dispose At the picnic, the children ______________ of their plastic bottles thoughtfully.

dispatch The post office ____________________ thousands of letters and parcels daily.

2 Colour the pairs of words that are synonyms. Use a different colour for each pair.

discuss	disaster	disguise	disease	disperse	disgust	disfigure
conceal	offend	spoil	debate	tragedy	sickness	scatter

3 Add prefixes to write the antonyms of these words. Choose from dis-, in- or un-.

loyal	____________	fortunate	____________
valid	____________	similar	____________
lawful	____________	interesting	____________
contented	____________	credible	____________
active	____________	graceful	____________

When a word ends in e, drop the e before adding a **suffix** beginning with a **vowel**.
*Examples: move, mov**able**; fame, fam**ous***
Keep the e if adding a suffix beginning with a consonant.
*Examples: move, move**ment**; safe, safe**ty***

4 Use the tip above to add suffixes to build nouns.

disfigure + ment	____________	discuss + ion	____________
dismiss + al	____________	disperse + al	____________
disturb + ance	____________	disapprove + al	____________
dispose + al	____________	dislocate + ion	____________
disengage + ment	____________	discover + y	____________

TARGETING SPELLING 6 © PASCAL PRESS ISBN 9781925490244

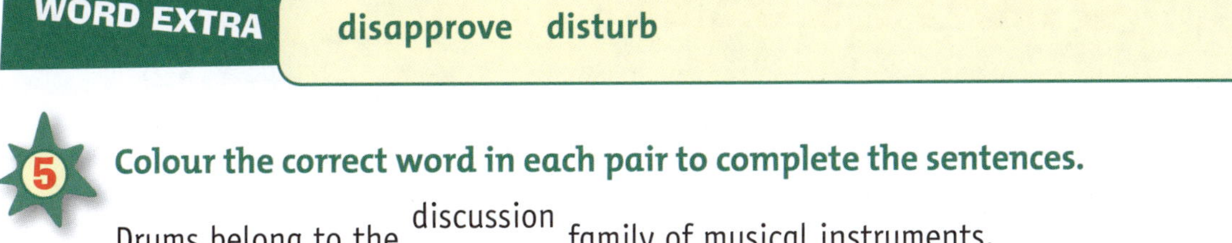

5 Colour the correct word in each pair to complete the sentences.

Drums belong to the discussion / percussion family of musical instruments.

I will soon need to discharge / recharge the battery in my mobile phone.

Sugar will dissolve / resolve in boiling water.

All Dad's travel dispenses / expenses are paid for by the company he works for.

Many music pieces for the violin were disposed / composed by an Italian named Vivaldi.

Pollutants are often gathered up in storm water and discharged / recharged into our waterways.

6 Match these verbs to their meanings. Use a dictionary to help you.

dis rupt →	prevent someone from concentrating on something; to sidetrack
dis tend	interrupt someone/something by causing a disturbance
dis suade	regard someone/something as having little value; to belittle
dis tract	pay no attention to; ignore
dis par age	swell; bulge; bloat; expand
dis in fect	recognise someone/something as different; pick out
dis re gard	discourage someone from taking a particular action
dis tin guish	get rid of germs; sterilise; decontaminate

Homonyms are words that have the same spelling or pronunciation, but mean different things in different contexts.
Example: ***sink*** *1. A stone will* ***sink*** *in water. 2. Wash the dishes in the* ***sink****.*

7 Write two sentences showing two different meanings for the words bear and drone.

1 ________________________________

2 ________________________________

1 ________________________________

2 ________________________________

8 Use the letters in this word to make new words. Write these words in columns in your notebook. Score your words and write your total score in the box.

disembarkation

Score 3 points for each 4-letter word.
Score 5 points for each 5-letter word.
Score 10 points for each 5+-letter word.

Silent Letters: k, g, w

Words with 'silent letters' are very old. The **k** in **knight**, the **g** in **gnome** and the **w** in **write** were once pronounced. They fell 'silent' because people found them hard to pronounce, but they became trapped in the spelling. Because what we *see* and what we *say* are different, we need to remember what they *look* like.

SEE & SAY

knack	knapsack	gnaw	gnat	writhe	wrangle
knead	knick-knack	gnash	gnarled	wreathe	wrestle
knobbly	knowledge	gnome		wretched	

1 Add endings to the words in bold to complete the sentences.

wrestle People worldwide enjoy watching the sport of ________________.

gnome The nursery sells garden ________________, stone statues and water fountains.

knead The chef ________________ the dough before rolling it out on a floured board.

gnaw My dog Toby is happily ________________ on a bone in the backyard.

wrangle The players are ________________ over whose turn it is to bat.

2 Colour the pairs of words that are synonyms. Use a different colour for each pair.

wretched	gnarled	wrestle	wrangle	writhe	knack	gnash
argue	squirm	grind	twisted	struggle	miserable	skill

WORD TRAPS

Don't confuse **wreath** (noun) and **wreathe** (verb).
A **wreath** is a ring of flowers and leaves. **Wreathe** means to cover or surround.
*Examples: I placed a **wreath** at the war memorial on ANZAC Day.*
*The valley is **wreathed** in morning mist.*

Don't confuse **wrung** and **rung**.
*Examples: He **wrung** his hands in anguish. The bell is **rung** at nine o'clock.*
*I climbed the ladder one **rung** at a time.*

3 Colour the correct word in the brackets.

Myra will [wring ring] the water out of the clothes and hang them out to dry.

[Need Knead] the [doe dough] and roll it out on a board dusted with [flower flour].

Connor placed a floral [wreath wreathe] at the base of the monument.

I have [wrung rung] the doorbell twice, but no one has answered.

The player [rested wrested] the ball out of the hands of his opponent.

My old wooden ladder has a broken [rung wrung].

You may leave when I [wring ring] the bell.

TARGETING SPELLING 6 © PASCAL PRESS ISBN 9781925490244

WORD EXTRA knuckles written

UNIT 3

Using your dictionary, write two other words beginning with kn, gn and wr then write a sentence about one word from each pair.

kn	gn	wr

Words (of French origin) may end in gn where the g is 'silent'. Match these words to their meanings.

foreign	a task/piece of work allocated to someone; job; chore
campaign	belonging to a different country; alien; strange; unknown
ensign	gentle and kind; warm-hearted; non-harmful
assignment	a bubbly white wine produced in France
champagne	a series of actions planned to achieve a goal (e.g. military, election)
align	to speak about someone in a spiteful way; insult; put down
benign	to place or arrange things in a straight line
malign	a flag/banner used particularly by an army/navy to show nationality

Write a short imaginative piece about Marcello and his donkey. Write in the third person and in the present tense. Here is an idea to get you started.

Marcello is leading his donkey Dobbin along a dusty road. The donkey is small and thin with knobbly knees and a wicked gleam in his eye. Marcello has wrapped a wreath of gum leaves around Dobbin's ears. Dobbin is carrying a strange cargo — knapsacks filled with hand-carved knick-knacks and garden gnomes!

Prefixes: ob-, per-

The **prefix ob-** means 'against'. In Latin, ***struo structus*** = *to build*, so ***ob**struct* = *to build a barrier against*.
The **prefix per-** means 'through'. In Latin, ***spiro*** = *I breathe*, so ***per**spire* = *to breathe (moisture) out through the skin*.

SEE & SAY

object	obscure	obstacle	perfect	permit	perspire
obstruct	obsolete	obnoxious	perform	persuade	perceive
obtain	observe	obvious	perfume	persist	personnel

1 Add endings to the words in bold to complete the sentences.

perspire The marathon runner crossed the line exhausted and ________________.

obtain The pilot ________________ clearance to land from the flight control tower.

perfect The Olympian executed his first dive ________________.

permit Weather ________________, the tennis match will go ahead as planned.

obscure Our view of the sea was ________________ by tall pine trees on the shoreline.

observe The coach is closely ________________ the new player's ball-handling skills.

2 Colour the pairs of words that are synonyms. Use a different colour for each pair.

obscure	permit	obnoxious	perceive	obstacle	persuade	obsolete
nasty	coax	understand	allow	outdated	unclear	barrier

3 Change these verbs to nouns by adding -ion or -ity. *(For help, refer to the Tips in Unit 1.)*

object ____________________ persuade ____________________

personal ____________________ perfect ____________________

observe ____________________ perspire ____________________

obstruct ____________________ obscure ____________________

An interesting change is made to **verbs** ending in **-eive** before adding **-ion** to form a **noun**, and **-ive** to form an **adjective**. First, replace the **ive** with **pt**, then add **-ion** or **-ive**.
*Example: percei**ve**, percep**tion**, percep**tive***

4 Using the tip above, change these verbs to nouns and adjectives.

	Noun	Adjective
perceive		
deceive		
receive		

TARGETING SPELLING 6 © PASCAL PRESS ISBN 9781925490244

WORD EXTRA symbol system

UNIT 4

Don't confuse **personnel**, **personal** and **personable**.
Personnel is a group of people employed in a particular organisation.
Personal describes something that is private to a particular person.
Personable describes a person who is pleasing in appearance and manner.

5 Join the syllables to read these words. Match the words to their meanings.

ob stin ate	building equipped with powerful telescopes to look at stars/planets
per pet ū al	relevant or appropriate to a particular matter
ob ser va tor y	stubborn; refusing to change one's mind; inflexible
ob lig a tor y	upright or vertical; at an angle of 90 degrees to another line/surface
per spect ive	never-ending or changing; long-lasting; enduring; permanent
ob serv ant	1. able to show height, width and depth in drawing; 2. point of view
per tin ent	watchful or alert; quick to notice details; sharp-eyed
per pen dic ū lar	required by law or some other rule; compulsory

6 Build adjectives by adding -ive or -able. *(Remember: de becomes s.)*

objection	______________	observe	______________
persuade	______________	obstruct	______________
person	______________	perceive	______________

7 Add vowels to mend the broken words. Use the clues to help you.
(Hint: All vowels in a word are the same)

C __ T __ M __ R __ N	a twin-hulled vessel
__ L __ V __ N	number in a cricket side
S __ CC __ MB	to give in to; to surrender
C __ R __ V __ N	a house on wheels
WR __ GGL __ NG	moving like a worm
__ LM __ N __ C	yearly book of events
K __ NN __ L	house for a dog
B __ N __ N __	type of fruit
SC __ BB __ RD	sheath to hold a sword
N __ V __ RTH __ L __ SS	besides; not withstanding; but

How many words can you remember?

Go back and choose any *See and Say* list. Read through it twice, focusing on how the words look and sound. Write as many words as you can remember in your notebook. Check how many you have written correctly and enter your score here. ☐

Prefixes: de-

The **prefix** de- means 'from' or 'down'. In Latin, ***scando scansus*** = *I climb*, so ***descend*** = *to climb down*; ***scribo scriptus*** = *I write*, so ***describe*** = *to write down*.
NOTE: In the first part of the *See and Say* list, the de- is pronounced as a 'schwa' sound **(duh)** e.g. ***duh****vise*. In the second part of the list, the de- is pronounced with a short vowel sound, e.g. ***dĕ****licate*.

SEE & SAY

despise	destroy	descend	decade	devastate	desperate
devise	deprive	devour	delegate	delicate	desolate
device	describe	detergent	detonate	definite	destitute

1 Choose a word from the *See and Say* list to complete the sentences.

The wings of a butterfly are beautiful but ______________________.

There are ten years in a ______________________.

Most people add ______________________ to hot water to wash the dishes.

The tsunami ______________________ed everything in its path.

One bomb exploded, but the second one failed to ______________________.

2 Colour the pairs of words that are synonyms. Use a different colour for each pair.

despise	definite	desolate	delicate	detonate	devour	deprive
ignite	hate	withhold	eat	sure	fragile	lonely

3 Add -ion to build nouns. *(Think about any rules or tips that may apply.)*

desperate ______________________

devastate ______________________

delegate ______________________

deprive ______________________

delete ______________________

desolate ______________________

define ______________________

determine ______________________

detonate ______________________

destitute ______________________

WORD TRAPS

Don't confuse **devise** (verb) and **device** (noun).
To **devise** something is to plan or invent something by careful thought (e.g. a timetable, a training schedule).
A **device** is a gadget, machine or other useful invention (e.g. a remote control device).

4 Build adverbs by adding -ly.

delicate ______________________

desperate ______________________

delightful ______________________

definite ______________________

desirable ______________________

deliberate ______________________

TARGETING SPELLING 6 © PASCAL PRESS ISBN 9781925490244

WORD EXTRA delete develop

UNIT 5

5 Complete this table of verbs.

	Add -s or -es	Add -ing	Add -ed
destroy			
detonate			
despise			
devour			
devastate			

6 Complete the words by adding the prefix de-. Join them to words of similar meaning.

___lay	delay	protect	___feat	________	unhappy
___flect	________	reduce	___frost	________	oppose
___cree	________	divert	___jected	________	conquer
___fend	________	postpone	___fy	________	shy
___crease	________	order	___mure	________	thaw

7 Read the following article. Circle the ten spelling mistakes then write the words correctly.

Birthdays are a time for celerbration and reflektion. A time to look back over the passed munths of your life; to ponder the ups and downs, and the highs and lows of your year. What knowlage have you gained? What new skills? Have you taken up a new hobbe or learned to play a musickle instrament? What people have left your life, or enterd it for the first time? There is so much to look back on — maybe with pride, maybe with sadness. What have you acheevd both inside your school and outside, and what are your goals for the next year of your life?

8 Write a short paragraph to answer some of the above questions about your past year.

Prefixes: inter-, trans-

The **prefix inter-** means 'between' or 'among'.
Example: People talk among themselves or ***inter****act with each other.*
(Words with a French origin begin with *enter*, e.g. ***enter****tain*.)
The **prefix trans-** means 'across' or 'from side to side'.
Examples: ***trans****port is to carry across;* ***trans****mit is to send across*

SEE & SAY

interact	interrupt	intervene	transact	transport	transmit
interfere	interject	interview	transfer	translate	transmission
intercept	intersect	interval	transform	transit	transparent

1 Choose a word from the *See and Say* list to complete these sentences. Add endings where necessary.

I am reading a Greek play, which has been ____________________ into English.

Rain ____________________ play on centre court.

There will a short ____________________ between Act 1 and Act 2 of our play.

Many goods are ____________________ all over Australia by road and rail.

It is during the pupa stage that the caterpillar ____________________ into a butterfly.

2 Complete this table of verbs.

	Add -s or -es	Add -ing	Add -ed
intervene			
intercept			
interfere			
transmit			
translate			
transfer			

3 Add -ion to build nouns. *(Think about any rules or tips that may apply.)*

interact ____________________ transact ____________________

interrupt ____________________ transform ____________________

intersect ____________________ translate ____________________

interject ____________________ transport ____________________

intervene ____________________ transit ____________________

4 Unscramble these watercrafts. Start with the letter in bold.

hpi**s** ____________ tr**f**a ____________ ctah**y** ____________ a**c**oen ____________

hgn**d**iy ____________ **c**tmnraaaa ____________ ya**k**ka ____________

WORD EXTRA

outburst outbreak

TARGETING SPELLING 6 © PASCAL PRESS ISBN 9781925490244

UNIT 6

5 Add inter- or trans- to complete the words in bold.

We are going ________**state** for our summer holidays.

The first heart ________**plant** was performed in 1968 in Sydney.

The watchers stood ________**fixed** by the sight of whales breaching the water.

Graphs and diagrams are ________**spersed** throughout this science text.

The accident victim received a life-saving blood ________**fusion**.

6 Join the prefixes to the word base to write different words.

Prefixes	Base	Words	Prefixes	Base	Words	Prefixes	Base	Words
inter	**act**	________	inter	**cept**	________	inter	**ject**	________
re		________	ex		________	re		________
ex		________	con		________	pro		________
trans		________	per		________	in		________

7 Choose a word from each set above. Compose three sentences using your chosen words.

____

____

____

8 Add inter- to the following words, then match the words to their meanings.

________**cede** →	short break in proceedings; recess; music played during an interval
________**lace**	to act on behalf of someone who is in trouble
________**change**	the way two (or more) things have an effect on each other
________**lude**	system for sending messages within a building; intercommunication
________**com**	to exchange places; trade; switch; swap
________**play**	to weave in and out of each other; intertwine

WORD TRAPS

Don't confuse **transparent** and **translucent**.
A **transparent** object allows light to pass through it (e.g. air, a car's windscreen).
A **translucent** object allows some, but not all, light to pass through it (e.g. stained glass, sea water, ice).
Note: opaque objects allow no light to pass through them (e.g. door, football).

9 Join the syllables to read this list of words. Match the words to their meanings.

in ter sect ion →	electrical device used for changing one voltage to another
in ter mēd i ate	between or among countries across the world
in ter mit tent	the place where two streets meet
in ter rog a tive	coming between two things in time, place, or stage in life; midway
in ter nă tion al	to go above and beyond expectation; surpass; exceed
trans it or y	forming a question
trans form er	happening now and again; stopping and starting; irregular
trans cend	brief; lasting for a short time; transient

Prefixes: com-, con-

The **prefixes** con- and com- mean 'with' or 'together'. Many base words come from Latin. Examples: ***struo*** *= build (****con****struct = build; form together);* ***pare*** *= like (****com****pare = liken one with another)*

SEE & SAY

comply	compute	communicate	confer	consider	confiscate
complex	compere	complicate	confirm	condition	congratulate
complete	commend	compulsory	conserve	conscious	convalesce

Add endings to the words in bold to complete the sentences.

compute The PC (or personal ________________) is a must in every modern home.

complete The torch went out, leaving the cavers ________________ in the dark.

confirm Our teacher ________________ that our school camp will be at Kirra Beach.

construct Cory is ________________ a model of the Harbour Bridge with Lego blocks.

confiscate If you bring a mobile phone, it will be ________________ for the day.

Colour the pairs of words that are synonyms. Use a different colour for each pair.

comply	compulsory	consider	confiscate	compute	convalesce	conscious
ponder	calculate	recuperate	obey	required	aware	seize

REVIEW

When a verb ends in **e**, drop the **e** before adding **-ing** ***and*** before **suffixes** beginning with a **vowel**. *Example: compare, compar**ing**, compar**able***

When a **regular verb** ends in **y**, follow these simple rules:

1 Add **-ing** to all verbs ending in **y**. *Examples: play**ing**, carry**ing***

2 If the letter before the **y** is a vowel, just add **-s** or **-ed**. *Examples: **plays**, **played***

3 If the letter before the **y** is ***not*** a vowel, change **y** to **i** and add **-es** or **-ed**. *Examples: try, tries, tried*

Complete this table of verbs.

	Add -s or -es	Add -ing	Add -ed
complete			
comply			
congratulate			
convey			
communicate			
conserve			

WORD EXTRA compare construct

TARGETING SPELLING 6 © PASCAL PRESS ISBN 9781925490244

UNIT 7

4 **Homonyms are words that have different meanings in different contexts. Check the meanings of the words condition and complete. Write two sentences showing two different meanings for these words.**

1 ______________________

2 ______________________

1 ______________________

2 ______________________

5 **Add the missing nouns in these sentences. Construct the nouns by adding a suffix to the words in the box. Choose from -ion and -ence.**

congratulate	convalesce	complex	conserve	commend	confer

The main character has brown hair, blue eyes and a fair ______________.

The ______________ of energy will help in the battle against global warming.

The teachers attended a ______________ on emerging trends in education.

One soldier received a ______________ for selfless acts in the field of war.

After a short ______________, the policeman returned to active duty.

The mayor offered his ______________s to athletes competing in the Olympic Games.

6 **Write adjectives by adding suffixes to these words. Choose from -able, -al and -ive.**

commend ______________ construct ______________

condition ______________ compare ______________

conceal ______________ consider ______________

continue ______________ console ______________

7 **Write a paragraph about the ways in which people communicate with each other. Don't forget the importance of body language.**

____

____

____

____

____

____

____

____

____

____

____

UNIT 8

Latin Roots: mitto missus, pes pedis

Many English words have their roots in the ancient language of Latin. Knowing the origins of words helps us to understand both meaning and spelling. *Examples:* ***dis** = away, **mitto missus** = send,* so ***dismiss** = to send away;* ***centi** = 100, **pes pedis** = foot,* so ***centipede** = a hundred feet*

SEE & SAY

commit	remiss	mission	pedal	pedestrian	centipede
permit	dismiss	intermission	pedestal	expedition	millipede
remit	missile	intermittent	pedlar	impede	stampede

Choose a word from the *See and Say* list to complete each sentence. Add endings where necessary.

You are not ____________ to take your backpack into the museum.

Rocks were scattered everywhere, ____________ our progress through the forest.

____________ have long, thin bodies and many pairs of legs.

The crime was ____________ around midnight on the 5th.

Keegan is ____________ fast down the path on his new bike.

TIPS

1 When a **verb** ends in **mit**, double the **t** before adding **-ing**, **-ed** or a suffix beginning with a vowel. *Examples: ad**mit**, ad**mitting**, ad**mitted**, ad**mittance***

2 Before adding **-ion** to form a **noun**, change the **t** to **ss**. *Example: ad**mit**, ad**mission***

Add prefixes to the word base mit to write different verbs. Using Tip 1 above, then add -ing and -ed.

com- e- sub- **mit** trans- ad- per- re-

	Add -ing	Add -ed
admit	admitting	admitted

3 Using Tip 2 above, change these verbs to nouns.

commit ____________ remit ____________

permit ____________ submit ____________

transmit ____________ emit ____________

WORD EXTRA emit transmit

TARGETING SPELLING 6 © PASCAL PRESS ISBN 9781925490244

Colour the pairs of words that are synonyms. Use a different colour for each pair.

pedal	permit	impede	expedition	pedestrian	intermission	remiss
block	walker	lever	careless	interval	allow	journey

Don't confuse pedal and peddle.
To **pedal** is to turn the pedals of a bike with your feet.
To **peddle** is to sell goods to individual buyers (e.g. eBay).
A person who **peddles** goods is a **pedlar**.

Add the missing letters to mend the broken words.

The earliest **miss** _ _ _ _ used for hunting were arrows, spears and boomerangs.

It was _ _ **miss** of me not to bring a hat and a bottle of water on our long trek.

I asked the teacher's _ _ _ **miss** _ _ _ to leave the room.

The beautiful marble statue stands on an old stone **ped** _ _ _ _ _.

You can cross the street safely at a **ped** _ _ _ _ _ _ _ crossing.

Loud claps of thunder caused the frightened horses to _ _ _ _ **ped** _.

Join the syllables to read this list of words. Match the words to their meanings.

miss ive	a four-footed animal
im ped i ment	a government representative sent on a special mission; diplomat
ped om ē ter	a letter, especially a long or official one; message; communiqué
dis miss ive	an obstruction to doing something; obstacle; barrier; handicap
bī ped	to make something happen sooner or more quickly; speed up
quad rū ped	a device for recording the number of steps a person takes
e miss ar y	showing something as unworthy of notice; scornful; offhand
ex ped ite	a two-legged creature

Use the letters in this word to make new words. Write these words in columns in your notebook. Score your words and write your total score in the box.

pedestrians

Score 3 points for each 4-letter word.
Score 5 points for each 5-letter word.
Score 10 points for each 5+-letter word.

How many words can you remember?

Go back and choose any *See and Say* list. Read through it twice, focusing on how the words look and sound. Write as many words as you can remember in your notebook. Check how many you have written correctly and enter your score here.

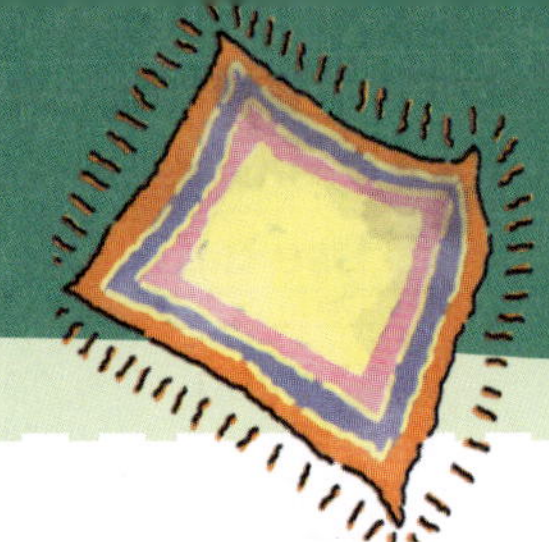

1 Name the pictures.

2 Complete this table of verbs. *(Apply any rules or tips.)*

	Add -s or -es	Add -ing	Add -ed
dismiss			
commit			
deprive			
comply			
disfigure			
pedal			

3 Write antonyms using the prefixes un-, im-, in- or dis-.

_____locate _____credit _____considerate

_____complicated _____delicate _____embark

_____patient _____interrupted _____definite

_____complete _____conscious _____conditional

4 Add -ion or -ence to build nouns. *(Apply any rules or tips.)*

imitate ______________ indulge ______________

observe ______________ perspire ______________

permit ______________ immunise ______________

interfere ______________ transmit ______________

obstruct ______________ transfer ______________

convalesce ______________ commend ______________

5 Add the missing letters to mend the broken words. Use the clues to help you.

one person	ind _ v _ d _ _ _	breathe in	_ _ h _ l _
debate an issue	disc _ _ _	wriggle or squirm	wri _ _ _
coax	per _ _ _ d _	used to wash dishes	de _ _ r _ _ _ t
to build	con _ _ r _ _ t	to copy	im _ _ a _ _
lower in quality	inf _ r _ _ _	a ring of flowers	_ _ ea _ _

TARGETING SPELLING 6 © PASCAL PRESS ISBN 9781925490244

6 Write one-word answers to match the word meanings.

word describing something that can be seen through	**trans**__________
something that can be thrown	**miss**__________
something that hides a person's appearance	**dis**__________
place where two streets cross each other	**inter**__________
required by law	**com**__________
something that gets in your way	**ob**__________
to break into someone's conversation	**inter**__________
to be aware of everything around you	**con**__________
the base on which a statue might stand	**ped**__________
happening now and again; starting and stopping	**inter**__________

7 Write words to match the meanings. *(Hint: The words begin with de- or per-.)*

__________	to try to get someone to do something; to coax
__________	to ruin completely; to devastate
__________	to climb down
__________	to act, sing or dance on stage
__________	to eat hungrily or greedily
__________	people who work for an organisation; staff
__________	to hate; dislike greatly
__________	a sweet aroma; scent
__________	to sweat
__________	to explain what something is like

8 Circle the spelling mistakes. Write them correctly in the box.

The first modin Olympic Games were held in Greece in 1896. At that time, nine sports were contested. Over the passed one hundred years, many sports have been added and remooved from the Olympic program. Only five sports have been contested at evry summer Olympic Games: swimming, athletics, cycling, gymnasticks and fencing.

Australia's Olympic team has grown from one competer in 1904 to 422 in Rio de Janeiro in 2016 with representatives in all 26 sports.

Frendly rivalry has long existed between Australia and the USA in the swimmming pool. Ian Thorpe is Australia's most prolific medalist, having won a total of five gold medals, three silva and one bronze in two Olympic Games.

Michael Phelps of the USA is acklaimed as the greatest swimmer of all time. He has won a staggring 23 gold medals in four Olympic Games.

Suffixes: -ate, -ise

The **verb-forming suffixes** -ate and -ise mean 'to make or do something'. Other verb-forming suffixes used in this way are -en *(harden)* and -fy *(beautify)*.

SEE & SAY

operate	estimate	separate	advertise	organise	exercise
investigate	excavate	populate	apologise	recognise	terrorise
irritate	navigate	nominate	criticise	minimise	analyse

1 Choose a word from the *See and Say* list to complete each sentence. Add endings where necessary.

A team of engineers are ____________________ a tunnel under the river.

Declan ____________________ for knocking my drink bottle over.

The pilot, with his ____________________ beside him, set out on a flight to Antarctica.

The police are ____________________ the cause of an accident involving two motorbikes.

The athletes are ____________________ in the gym to build stamina and muscular strength.

2 Colour the pairs of words that are synonyms. Use a different colour for each pair.

organise	advertise	irritate	estimate	analyse	nominate	minimise
examine	guess	arrange	promote	name	lessen	annoy

3 Build nouns by adding -ion or -ism. *(Apply any rules and tips.)*

operate ____________________ organise ____________________

critic ____________________ populate ____________________

navigate ____________________ terror ____________________

estimate ____________________ nominate ____________________

excavate ____________________ irritate ____________________

4 The suffix -ise is added to many words to form a verb. Add -ise to these words then match them to their meanings.

critic ise — to punish; put at a disadvantage

public_____ — to bring to an end; conclude; complete; finish up

maxim_____ — to find fault with someone/something

idol_____ — to become fully aware of something; clearly understand

penal_____ — to make as large or great as possible; make the best use of

improv~~e~~_____ — to make something widely known to people

real_____ — to create and perform something without preparation

final_____ — to admire greatly; adore; hero-worship

When you add –ise to words ending in c, the c becomes a soft c and is pronounced as an s.

TARGETING SPELLING 6 © PASCAL PRESS ISBN 9781925490244

WORD EXTRA energy chemist

5 Write the verbs from which these nouns have been built.

recognition	recognise	analysis	
apology		summary	
advertisement		investigator	
terrorist		energy	
irritant		publicity	

6 Place a syllable in each box to spell the missing words in these sentences.

London is a large city with a **p**___ of 8.6 million people.
The surgeon performed an **o**___ on her patient.
I **e**___ daily to keep myself fit and healthy.
I saw an **a**___ in the window for a new electronic game.
I owe my friend an **a**___ for losing his favourite ball.

7 Match each verb to its meaning by writing its number in the box. Use a dictionary to help you.

1 vacate	2 hesitate	3 vibrate	4 radiate
5 activate	6 graduate	7 duplicate	8 inflate

☐ quiver, shake or tremble
☐ make an exact copy of
☐ fill with air or gas; pump up
☐ pause when unsure; hang back
☐ successfully complete a course of study
☐ leave somewhere; exit or depart from
☐ put something into action; start up
☐ send out rays of light or heat

8 Nouns are often formed by adding -ion. Write the noun form of the verbs above.

1	5
2	6
3	7
4	8

9 Unscramble these Olympic sports. Start with the letter in bold.

smiminwg	ymst**g**ncisa	lethc**a**ist
ornigw	gcclyni	chyrre**a**

Word Endings: o

Words ending in **o** have their origins in Latin. The influence of Italian on our language remains great. *Auto*, *cappuccino*, *radio* and *risotto* are all familiar words in English. Many musical instruments and musical terms are Italian. *Examples: piano, piccolo, cello, tempo, largo (slow), presto (fast), concerto, soprano*

SEE & SAY

solo	photo	studio	hero	tomato	tornado
silo	piano	stereo	echo	embargo	avocado
cello	radio	cappuccino	potato	cargo	volcano

1 Name the pictures.

			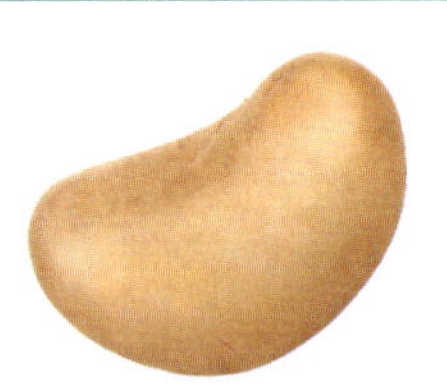	

Most words ending in **o** are **nouns**. Some add **-s** to form their plural, and some add **-es**. *Examples: pianos, potatoes*
Some drop the **o** before adding endings, and some don't.
Examples: volcanic, soloist

Here's a tip to remember how to spell cappuccino. U is the cup in the middle. If you have 2 cups of coffee (CC), you must say please (PP) twice!
c a P P U CC i n o

2 Complete this table of verbs.

Add -s		Add -es	
solo	silo	hero	echo
cello	piano	potato	tomato
photo	studio	cargo	tornado
radio	avocado	volcano	mosquito

3 Add to the words you know ending in o. Match them to their meanings.

bravo	international exhibition	tempo	Italian ice-cream
expo	cotton cloth	poncho	sauce served with pasta
calico	round, stringed instrument	dingo	rhythm or beat in music
polo	Well done!	gelato	cloak with a hole for the head
banjo	game played on horseback	pesto	Australian wild dog

TARGETING SPELLING 6 © PASCAL PRESS ISBN 9781925490244

WORD EXTRA search worst

UNIT 10

Colloquial language is chatty and informal — the type we use in our everyday communication with each other. *Examples:* ***uni*** *= university;* ***snags*** *= sausages;* ***footy*** *= football;* ***chook*** *= chicken;* ***bushie*** *= country person*

4 Match each verb to its meaning by writing its number in the box. Use a dictionary to help you.

1 speedo	2 gusto	3 combo	4 pronto
5 arvo	6 cheerio	7 aggro	8 kilo

☐	with enthusiasm and enjoyment	☐	quickly; promptly
☐	car's odometer to measure speed	☐	the afternoon
☐	a combination of different foods	☐	a kilogram
☐	goodbye; little red sausage	☐	aggressive behaviour

For the music buffs
What are the following?
- soprano
- alto
- falsetto
- crescendo
- decrescendo
- pianissimo
- moderato
- presto
- lento
- concerto
- oratorio

5 Circle the spelling mistakes. Write them correctly in the box.

The cello is a member of the string family of musickle instruments. Like the violin, it has four strings stretched over a *bridge* anchored at the top by four pegs. The player turns these pegs to losen or tighten the strings to *tune* their instrument so that the sounds blend togetha and are plesant to the ear. Like the violin, the cello is played by moving a *bow* across the strings. Sometimes the strings are pluckt by the player for a partickula effect.

The cello has a deep, rich tonal qualaty and is often played as a solo instrument accompanyd by piano. The cello also forms part of a *trio*, *quartet* or full *orchestra*.

6 Do some research of your own about one of these musical instruments: piano, piccolo or banjo. Write notes about your research as bullet points. Write in sentences.

Suffixes: -fy

The **suffix** **-fy** means 'to make' or 'to do'. To *clarify* is *to make something clear*; to *simplify* is *to make something simple or easier to do.*

signify	modify	justify	defy	mystify	testify
simplify	notify	identify	intensify	verify	clarify
magnify	qualify	terrify	horrify	pacify	classify

1 Colour the pairs of words that are synonyms. Use a different colour for each pair.

verify	mystify	classify	notify	intensify	defy	identify
tell	increase	oppose	confirm	recognise	sort	bewilder

When a word ends in **fy**, just add **-ing**, but change the **y** to **i** before adding **-es**, **-ed** or **-er**.
*Example: justify, justify**ing**, justif**ies**, justif**ied**, justif**ier***

2 Complete this table of verbs. In the fourth column, say *who* or *what* would perform this action by adding **-er**.

	Add -es	Add -ing	Add -ed	Add -er
classify				
qualify				
magnify				
modify				
pacify				

TIP

Interesting changes are made to **verbs** ending in **-fy** before adding **-tion**.
First, replace the **y** with **ic**, then add **ā** and **-tion**, e.g. *classify* → *classif**ication***.
Other **nouns** are formed by replacing **fy** with **ty**, e.g. *dignify* → *digni**ty***.

3 Using the tips above, change these verbs to nouns by adding **-tion** and **-ity**.

	Add -tion	Add -ity
clarify		
identify		
intensify		
qualify		

WORD EXTRA

fulfil seldom

TARGETING SPELLING 6 © PASCAL PRESS ISBN 9781925490244

UNIT 11

4 Using different colours, highlight the words that belong in the same 'family'.

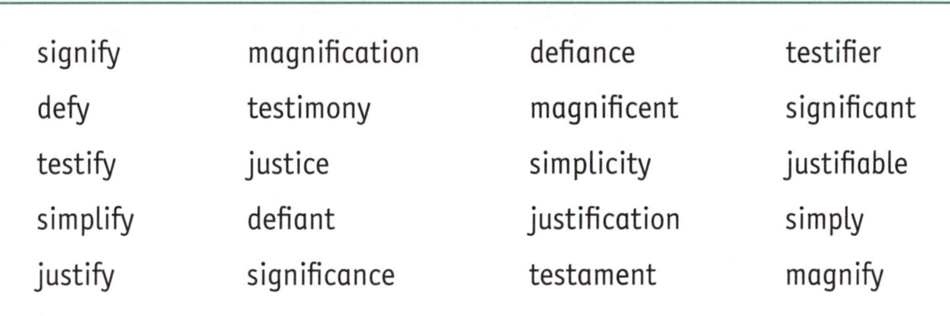

signify	magnification	defiance	testifier
defy	testimony	magnificent	significant
testify	justice	simplicity	justifiable
simplify	defiant	justification	simply
justify	significance	testament	magnify

5 Add endings to the words in bold to complete the sentences.

quality The ____________________ required are: skill, honesty and punctuality.

terrify Being stranded metres high in a cable car was ____________________.

identify Scientists have ____________________ a new species of peacock spider.

defiant The protesters waved their banners ____________________ outside Parliament.

mystify Residents were ____________________ by the sudden appearance of a sinkhole.

6 Build your word knowledge. Match these verbs and their meanings.

beaut i fy	to become hard; set; freeze; thicken; stiffen
rect i fy	to improve the appearance of something; decorate; embellish; adorn
cert i fy	to make pure; cleanse; decontaminate
spec i fy	to put right; repair; fix up; remedy
solid i fy	to make someone so frightened they cannot move
pur i fy	to confirm something; guarantee; verify; endorse
fals i fy	to state something clearly and precisely; detail; define; itemise
petr i fy	to make something incorrect, especially to deceive someone; to fake

7 Write two sentences showing two different meanings for the words second and deck.

1 ____

2 ____

1 ____

2 ____

8 Use the letters in this word to make new words. Write these words in columns in your notebook. Score your words and write your total score in the box.

instrumental

Score 3 points for each 4-letter word.
Score 5 points for each 5-letter word.
Score 10 points for each 5+-letter word.

'Soft' g, c

When **g** is followed by an **e**, **i** or **y**, it has a 'soft' sound (**j**).
Examples: ***gentle, giant, gym***
When **c** is followed by an **e**, **i** or **y**, it has a 'soft' sound (**s**).
Examples: ***cent, city, cyclone***

SEE & SAY

arrange	urgent	oblige	accident	police	cereal
agenda	engine	emerge	incident	policy	celebrate
digital	region	legend	terrace	success	century

1 Add endings to the words in bold to complete the sentences.

arrange Phillip is ____________________ the chairs in rows of ten.

terrace We saw ____________________ of rice fields on our trip through Asia.

digital Old movies are often ____________________ re-mastered.

century The stone castle, now crumbling, was built ____________________ ago.

celebrate The Porter twins are ____________________ their eleventh birthday.

urgent The stranded mountain climber needed help ____________________.

2 Write these nouns in plural form.

agenda	engine	policy	success	cereal
__________	__________	__________	__________	__________

3 Colour the pairs of words that are synonyms. Use a different colour for each pair.

region	legend	accident	cereal	engine	emerge	policy
mishap	appear	tale	plan	area	grain	motor

4 Complete this table of present and past tense verbs.

	Add -s	Add -ing	Add -ed
arrange			
oblige			
celebrate			
police			
emerge			

WORD EXTRA centre general

TARGETING SPELLING 6 © PASCAL PRESS ISBN 9781925490244

In Latin, *centum = 100*. Match each word to its meaning by writing its number in the box. Use a dictionary to help you.

UNIT 12

1 cent	2 centenary	3 centurion	4 percentage
5 centipede	6 bicentennial	7 centigrade	8 centenarian

	a person of one hundred years or more		an officer commanding one hundred men
	an insect with many pairs of feet		a coin equal to one hundredth of a dollar
	a number out of one hundred; %		a heat scale from 0 to 100 degrees
	celebrating two hundred years		the hundredth anniversary of an event

Build adjectives by adding suffixes. (*Apply the e rule.*)

region + al	__________	legend + ary	__________
success + ful	__________	incident + al	__________
celebrate + ory	__________	centre + al	__________
emerge + ent	__________	polit + ic + al	__________

Cross out (×) the incorrect word in the brackets.

There were many amusing [incidents accidents] during the movie.

The police responded to an [emergent urgent] call for help.

We live in the 21st [centenary century].

We had to battle through rugged [terrace terrain] to reach the summit.

It is always a good [police policy] to save some of your earnings.

Join the syllables to read this list of words. Match the words to their meanings. Use a dictionary to help you.

lī cence	an unexpected, often serious, situation requiring immediate action
cō in cid ence	official permission to do something, e.g. driving licence
ē mer gen cy	to solve a puzzle; work out; break the code
cyl in der	people born and living at the same time, e.g. the 1990s
gen er ā tion	the surprising occurrence of two things at the same time
dē cī pher	a spice obtained from the bark of a tree and used in cooking
cin na mon	a tube-shaped object with circular ends

How many words can you remember?

Go back and choose any *See and Say* list. Read through it twice, focusing on how the words look and sound. Write as many words as you can remember in your notebook. Check how many you have written correctly and enter your score here. ☐

Suffixes: -or, -ar

The **suffixes -or** and **-ar** (like **-er**) mean 'one who' or 'that which'.
One who survives is a *survivor*; that which senses things is a *sensor*.
One who tells lies is a *liar*; that which is the same is *similar*.
We tend to 'slur' over the end syllable in words.
This slurring produces the **schwa** sound **(uh)**. *Examples:* We say *tenuh*, but we write *tenor*; we say *scholuh*, but we write *scholar*.

You will need to carefully match what you see with what you say.

SEE & SAY

tenor	censor	survivor	liar	regular	spectacular
vendor	sculptor	governor	scholar	singular	perpendicular
sensor	solicitor	commentator	nectar	similar	binoculars

1 **Write these nouns in plural form.**

governor ________ tenor ________ scholar ________ sculptor ________ liar ________

2 **Colour the pairs of words that are synonyms. Use a different colour for each pair.**

vendor	tenor	regular	similar	scholar	solicitor	spectacular
usual	lawyer	student	eye-catching	seller	alike	singer

3 **Add -ly to form adverbs.**

regular ________ scholar ________
similar ________ spectacular ________
popular ________ peculiar ________

WORD TRAPS

Don't confuse **sensor** and **censor**.
A **sensor** is a device that detects changes like heat, movement and light and responds to it.
A **censor** is a person who examines movies, plays and news reports to see if they are suitable for the public. Films have *censorship* ratings such as G (for general exhibition) and PG (parental guidance recommended).

4 **Write the base word. Add a suffix to the base word to form a noun.** ***(Note any rules.)***

sensor	sense	add **-tion**	sensation
sculptor	________	add **-ure**	________
governor	________	add **-ment**	________
survivor	________	add **-al**	________
instructor	________	add **-ion**	________
director	________	add **-ory**	________

TARGETING SPELLING 6 © PASCAL PRESS ISBN 9781925490244

WORD EXTRA author dollar

UNIT 13

5 **Complete this short quiz. Write one-word answers.**

a high male singing voice t________

one who tells lies l________

special magnifying glasses for two eyes b________

at the same time each day r________

count nouns are ______ or plural s________

one who comments/explains sporting events c________

a sweet liquid made into honey by bees n________

one who carves statues s________

one who writes stories a________

Add vowels to mend the broken words. Use the clues to help you.
(Hint: All vowels in a word are the same.)

J __ C __ R __ N D __ a large tree with blue, trumpet-shaped flowers

T __ P __ __ a cone-shaped tent traditionally made of skins

S __ L __ RY a fixed regular payment for work

R __ M __ M B __ R to recall something in your mind

PL __ C __ RD a large notice or poster

S __ PT __ MB __ R the ninth month of the year

DR __ M __ a play acted on stage, radio or television

S __ V __ NT __ __ N a number

__ L __ M __ NT an essential part of something

M __ SS __ SS __ PP __ a very long river in North America

Become an interviewer. Write five questions you would like to ask one of the following people: the Governor-General of Australia, a sports commentator, an earthquake survivor, a famous author.

1 ________________________________

2 ________________________________

3 ________________________________

4 ________________________________

5 ________________________________

Suffixes: -ive and Prefixes: mono-, bi-, micro-

The **adjective-forming suffix -ive** means 'able to'.
*Examples: attract**ive** = able to attract; impress**ive** = able to impress*
The **prefix mono-** means 'one', **bi-** means 'two' and **micro-** means 'very small'.

SEE & SAY

attractive	impressive	pensive	monopoly	bicycle	microscope
sensitive	imperative	expensive	monotone	biennial	microphone
intensive	expressive	productive	monologue	bilingual	microwave

1 Write these nouns in their plural form.

bicycle ______ microphone ______ monologue ______ microscope ______ monopoly ______

2 Build adverbs by adding -ly, and nouns by adding -ness or -ity.

	Adverbs (add -ly)	Nouns (add -ness or -ity)
attractive		
expressive		
impressive		
productive		
sensitive		
attentive		
pensive		

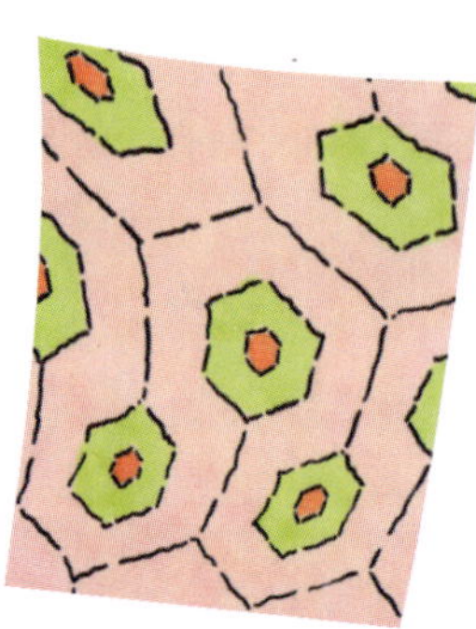

3 Colour the pairs of words that are synonyms. Use a different colour for each pair.

pensive	imperative	expensive	bicycle	intensive	selective	active
dear	choosy	thoughtful	busy	crucial	thorough	bike

4 Add prefixes to these adjectives to write antonyms. Choose from un- and in-.

attractive ______ sensitive ______
expensive ______ impressive ______
productive ______ active ______

WORD EXTRA active selective

TARGETING SPELLING 6 © PASCAL PRESS ISBN 9781925490244

mono = 1 **bi** = 2 **tri** = 3

UNIT 14

5 Add a number to complete these sentences. Use the prefixes as a clue.

A **biennial** event would occur every ____________ years.

A **tripod** is a stand with ____________ legs.

A **monologue** is spoken by ____________ person.

A **bilingual** person can speak ____________ languages.

A **trio** is a group of ____________ people.

A **bicycle** has ____________ wheels and a **tricycle** has ____________.

A **triennial** event would happen every ____________ years.

____________ person would **monopolise** a conversation.

A **triathlon** consists of ____________ sports — swimming, cycling and running.

A person speaking at only ____________ pitch is speaking in a **monotone**.

6 Circle the spelling mistakes. Write them correctly in the box.

The Eurovision Song Contest is an annule international TV song contest held particularly among members of the European Broadcasting Union. Singers from participating countries receive votes from both a panel of judges and the genral viewing public. It is a glittering, glamorus occasion with a large live audiance and millions of viewers across the world.

In 2015, Australia was invited to participate in the contest for the first time. Dami Im was chosen to sing for Australia in 2016, following her sucksess in the TV music compitition *The X Factor*. Dami made it through the semi-finals to reach the Grand Final, where she recieved a standing ovation for a spectacklar rendition of her song, 'Sound of Silence', which was speshly written for the contest. When all the votes were counted, Dami was awarded second place, bringing her worldwide recognishun.

7 Prepare a monologue to deliver to your classmates. Choose a topic of high interest to yourself, e.g. a hobby, a sport, or a local or world issue.

Prefixes: ex-, e-

The **prefix ex-** (and its variant **e-**) means 'out of' or 'from'.
In Latin, ***claudo clausus*** = *close*, so ***exclude*** = *to close out*;
lego lectus = *choose* or *read*, so ***elect*** = *to choose from*.

SEE & SAY

expel	exhale	experience	elect	elaborate	elevate
expire	extinct	extinguish	elapse	eliminate	element
explicit	exclude	extravagant	elastic	elongate	eligible

1 Add a noun suffix to the word in bold to complete each sentence. Choose from -ion, -ness, -ance or -y.

elect An ________________ for school captain will take place on 11 February.

extinguish Dad installed a fire ________________ on a wall in the kitchen.

expire Before I buy milk, I always check the ________________ date.

elevate Toowoomba has an ________________ of 600 metres above sea level.

extravagant The court of Louis XIV was one of luxury and ________________.

extinct An asteroid hitting Earth caused the ________________ of the dinosaurs.

2 Write the ex- and e- words.

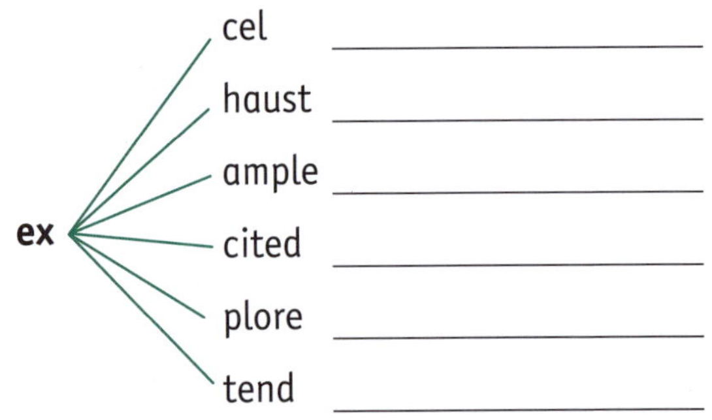

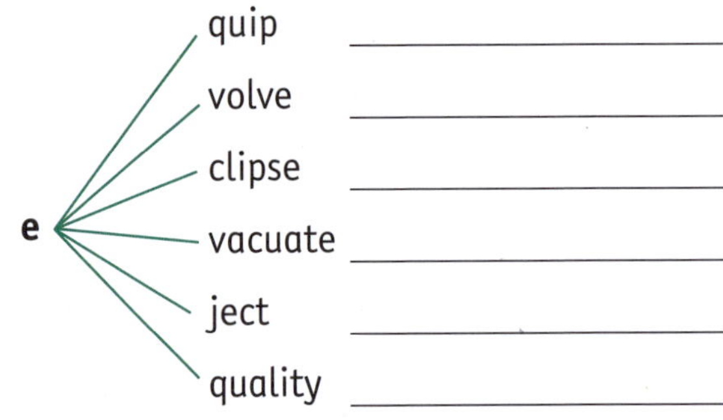

3 Colour the pairs of words that are synonyms. Use a different colour for each pair.

extinct	exclude	elapse	eliminate	eligible	expire	elevate
pass	discard	qualified	long-dead	die	raise	omit

4 Add the missing letters to mend the broken words.

El __ __ __ **ic** is used in dressmaking because it will stretch.

The Olympic closing ceremony was **el** __ **bor** __ __ __ and **extr** __ **v** __ **g** __ __ __.

After the semi-finals, six runners had been **el** __ **m** __ **n** __ __ **ed.**

Water is composed of two **el** __ **m** __ __ **ts:** hydrogen and oxygen.

Our trip to Antarctica was an unforgettable **exp** __ __ __ **en** __ __.

Grain is transported up into a silo by means of an **el** __ **v** __ **t** __ __.

WORD EXTRA

exhibit examine

TARGETING SPELLING 6 © PASCAL PRESS ISBN 9781925490244

Add the suffix -ion to build nouns.
(Hint: If you need help, check the tips in Unit 1.)

exhibit ____________	examine ____________
exclude ____________	exhale ____________
eliminate ____________	elevate ____________
evade ____________	evacuate ____________

Colour the correct word to complete each sentence.

The coach gave the keeper explicit / implicit instruction in how to defend the goal.

Ten minutes collapsed / elapsed before the start of the next boat race.

Her gold medal performance has expired / inspired us all to train even harder.

I would love to be included / excluded in the cricket team representing Australia.

It was hard to extinguish / distinguish the man's face in the fading light.

Join the syllables to read the words then match them to their meanings.
(ĕ = short vowel; ē = long vowel)

ex pĕr ĭ ment	full of energy and excitement; in high spirits; cheerful
ex pō sĭ tion	a test or trial to find out something
ex quĭs ĭte	a short trip, usually for a specific reason
ex term ĭn āte	gorgeous; stunning; delicate; beautiful
ex ūb er ant	perfect; ideal; being a good example to follow
ex cur sion	1. large public show of arts or trade goods; 2. a detailed explanation
ex ĕmp lar y	to get rid of something by destroying it

Add vowels to mend the broken words. Use the clues to help you.
(Hint: All vowels in a word are different)

V __ __ L __ T	a small purple flower; a shade of purple
C __ RC __ L __ R	shaped like a ring
S __ RFB __ __ RD	equipment used to ride the waves
C __ R __ __ S __ L	a merry-go-round
FR __ G __ L __	delicate; weak; easily broken
C __ ST __ M __ S	clothes worn by actors
D __ __ BL __ NG	multiplying by two
C __ M __ D __ __ N	a funny person
M __ D __ __ M	average; middle-sized
S __ SP __ NS __ __ N	a type of bridge hung over a deep, wide valley

Prefixes: en-

The **prefix en-** means 'within', 'in' or 'into'.
*Examples: **en**danger = to put in danger;*
***en**tangle = to get tangled within something*

SEE & SAY

endure	enchant	enlarge	entire	entreat	endeavour
endanger	endorse	enquire	entitle	entangle	envisage
entice	engrossed	enslave	ensue	entertain	environment

1 Add endings to the words in bold to complete the sentences.

endanger The Bengal tiger is an ______________________ species.

enquire The police are making ______________________ into the missing jewels.

entire The low-lying reef is ______________________ submerged at high tide.

entangle My fishing line became ______________________ in thick seaweed.

ensue In the ______________________ days, the quake victims faced many hardships.

entitle Her latest novel is ______________________ *The White Swans of Willoughby*.

2 Colour the pairs of words that are synonyms. Use a different colour for each pair.

enchant	envisage	endeavour	ensue	entreat	endorse	entire
try	beg	whole	support	delight	imagine	follow

en may be both a **prefix** and a **suffix**. As a **verb suffix**, it means 'to make' or 'to do',
so *stiff**en** = to make stiff; hard**en** = to make hard.*
The **suffix -en** may also be added to words to form **adjectives**. Here it means 'made of'.
*Example: wood**en** = made of wood*

3 Write the words from the word wheels.
Wheel 1: Join the prefix en-; Wheel 2: Join the suffix -en.

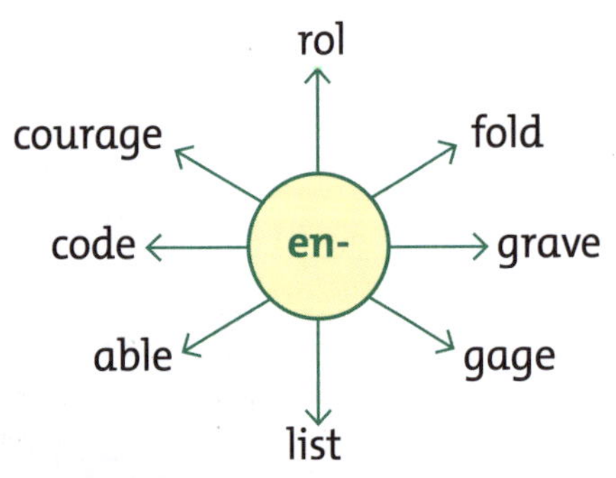

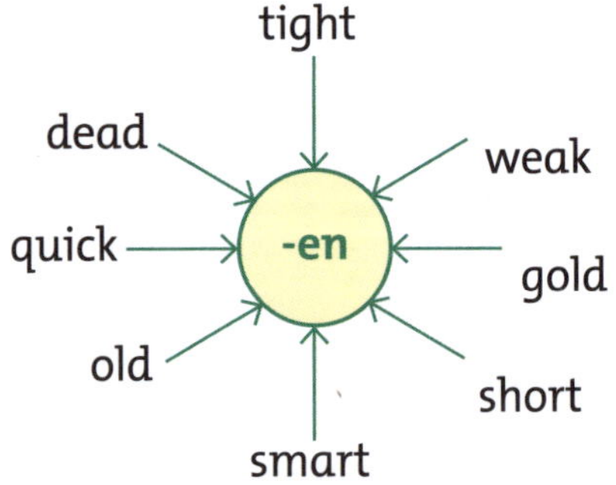

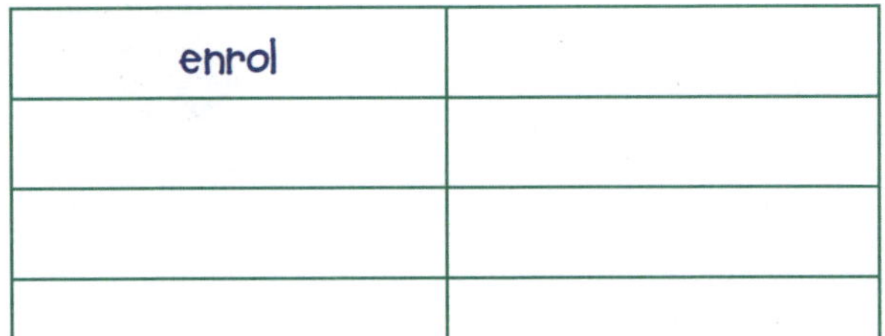

enrol	

tighten	

TARGETING SPELLING 6 © PASCAL PRESS ISBN 9781925490244

WORD EXTRA enforce enthralled

Don't confuse **ensure**, **insure** and **assure**.
Ensure means to make certain.
*Example: Please **ensure** you complete your project by Friday.*
Insure means to secure property against loss or damage.
*Example: Dad will **insure** his new car.*
Assure means to say something with certainty.
*Example: I **assure** you I will be home by five o'clock.*

4 Complete this table of verbs.

	Add -s	Add -ing	Add -ed
enchant			
entice			
endorse			
endure			
enthral			

When a **verb** ends in **e**, do not drop the **e** when adding a **suffix** beginning with a consonant. *Examples: engage**ment**, brave**ness**, mate**ship***

5 Build nouns by adding the suffix -ment to these verbs.

entertain ____________ enforce ____________

enlarge ____________ enchant ____________

endorse ____________ entice ____________

entitle ____________ entangle ____________

6 Write a brief paragraph about your favourite entertainment.

____

____

____

____

____

____

____

How many words can you remember?

Go back and choose any *See and Say* list. Read through it twice, focusing on how the words look and sound. Write as many words as you can remember in your notebook. Check how many you have written correctly and enter your score here. ☐

TARGETING SPELLING 6 © PASCAL PRESS ISBN 9781925490244

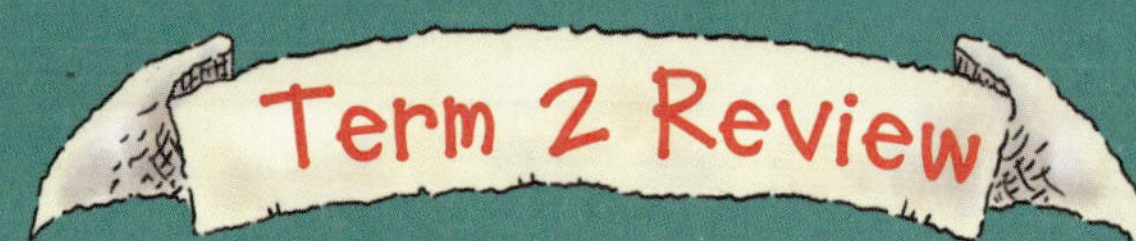

1 Name the pictures.

2 Write these nouns in plural form.

potato	______	apology	______	studio	______
policy	______	cargo	______	century	______
exercise	______	success	______	terrace	______
chemist	______	energy	______	hero	______

3 Add endings to these verbs. *(Apply any tips or rules.)*

Add -ing (present participle)		Add -ed (past participle)		Add -er or -or (to form nouns)	
recognise		signify		operate	
enthral		expel		classify	
terrify		censor		navigate	
separate		enquire		elevate	
entice		defy		advertise	

4 Write a synonym for each word using the letter clues.

lawyer	**s**______	alike	**s**______	motor	**en**______
100 years	**c**______	alone	**s**______	omit	**ex**______
writer	**a**______	cyclone	**t**______	image	**ph**______
100 cents	**d**______	stretchy	**el**______	ask	**en**______

TARGETING SPELLING 6 © PASCAL PRESS ISBN 9781925490244

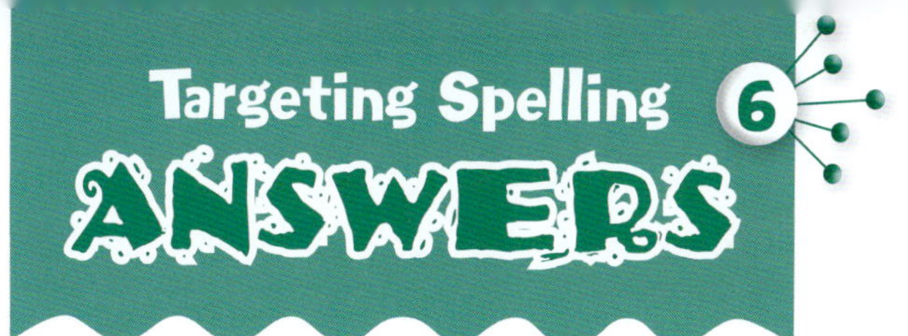

Unit 1

1 immunise, impose, inhale, inhabit, immaculate
2 indicates, indicating, indicated; imitates, imitating, imitated; inhales, inhaling, inhaled; immunises, immunising, immunised; indulges, indulging, indulged; impresses, impressing, impressed
3 impress, depress, compress, express; impose, depose, compose, expose
4 imitate-copy; implore-beg; immense-huge; indicate-point; immerse-dip; inferior-shoddy; indulge-pamper
5 invasion, immunisation, inhalation, indication, implosion, imposition, imitation, implementation
6 impossible, infertile, impolite, incorrect, undefeated, unimportant, unsure, improbable, infamous, insane, unlikely, inactive
7 impulsive: acting rashly without forethought; imposing: grand, striking, eye-catching; inhabitable: suitable to live in; impressive: causing admiration for quality or skill; indulgent: being over-generous; soft-hearted; inferior: lower in rank/quality; second-class; invasive: intruding on someone/something; imminent: about to happen; approaching; near

Unit 2

1 dislocating, discounted, diseases, discharging, disposed, dispatches
2 discuss-debate; disaster-tragedy; disguise-conceal; disease-sickness; disperse-scatter; disgust-offend; disfigure-spoil
3 disloyal, invalid, unlawful, discontented, inactive, unfortunate, dissimilar, uninteresting, incredible, disgraceful (ungraceful)
4 disfigurement, dismissal, disturbance, disposal, disengagement, discussion, dispersal, disapproval, dislocation, discovery
5 percussion, recharge, dissolve, expenses, composed, discharged
6 distend: swell; bulge; bloat, expand; dissuade: discourage someone from taking a particular action; distract: prevent someone from concentrating on something; to sidetrack; disparage: regard someone/something as having little value; to belittle; disinfect: get rid of germs; sterilise; decontaminate; disregard: pay no attention to; ignore; distinguish: recognise someone/something as different; pick out
7 Writing activity
8 Examples: 4-letter: amen, amid, ants, arms, arts, bait, bake, band, bane, bank, bark, barn, base, bask, bead, beak, beam, bean, bear, beat, bend, bent, best, bide, bike, bind, biro, bite, boat, bone, bore, born, brat, bred, brim, dame, dank, dare, dark, darn, dart, date, dear, dent, diet, dime, dine, dint, dire, dirk, dirt, disk, dome, dote, drab, earn, ears, east, edit, emit, item, kids, kind, kite, made, maid, main, make, mane, mark, mask, mast, mate, mean, meat, mine, mint, mist, mite, moan, moat, most, name, near, neat, nose, note, oaks, omen, omit, orbs, raid, rain, rake, rank, rant, rate, read, ream, rein, rent, rest, rink, rise, risk, road, roam, robe, rose, rote, sake, same, sand, sank, sate, send, sent, side, sink, sire, site, skid, skim, skin, skit, soak, some, sore, sort, stab, star, stem, take, tame, tank, task, teak, team, tear, tide, time, tire, toad, toes, tomb, tone, tore, torn, tram, trek, trim, trod

5-letter: abate, abode, adore, baker, basin, baste, beast, board, boast, bored, brain, brake, brand, bread, break, bream, bride, brink, brisk, broad, broke, drain, drake, drank, dream, drink, drone, knit, knob, knot, meant, merit, midst, miner, minor, miser, mitre, moist, named, raise, rinse, risen, siren, skate, smite, smoke, smote, snore, snort, stain, stair, stake, stand, stare, stark, steak, steam, stern, stink, stoke, stone, stork, storm, strap, strip, timid, tired, trade, train, tread, tribe, tries

5+ letters: amber, ardent, banker, banter, barked, basket, basted, braise, breast, embark, maiden, market, masked, master, mentor, modern, ration, stoked, stream, stride, strident, strike, strode, stroke, tanker, timber, timbre, tinder, tinker

Unit 3

1 wrestling, gnomes, kneaded, gnawing, wrangling
2 wretched-miserable; gnarled-twisted; wrestle-struggle; wrangle-argue; writhe-squirm; knack-skill; gnash-grind
3 wring; Knead, dough, flour; wreath; rung; wrested; rung; ring
4 Writing activity
5 campaign: a series of actions planned to achieve a goal; ensign: a flag/banner used particularly by an army/navy to show nationality; assignment: a task/piece of work allocated to someone; job; chore; champagne: a bubbly white wine produced in France; align: to place or arrange things in a straight line; benign: gentle and kind; warm-hearted; non-harmful; malign: to speak about someone in a spiteful way; insult; put down
6 Writing activity

Unit 4

1 perspiring, obtained, perfectly, permitting, obscured, observing
2 obscure-unclear; permit-allow; obnoxious-nasty; perceive-understand; obstacle-barrier; persuade-coax; obsolete-outdated
3 objection, personality, observation, obstruction, persuasion, perfection, perspiration, obscurity
4 perception, perceptive; deception, deceptive; reception, receptive
5 perpetual: never-ending or changing; long-lasting; enduring; permanent; observatory: building equipped with powerful telescopes to look at stars/planets; obligatory: required by law or some other rule; compulsory; perspective: 1. able to show height, width and depth in drawing; 2. point of view; observant: watchful or alert; quick to notice details; sharp-eyed; pertinent: relevant or appropriate to a parrticular matter; perpendicular: upright or vertical; at an angle of 90 degrees to another line/surface
6 objectionable, persuasive, personable, observable, obstructive, perceptive

7 catamaran, eleven, succumb, caravan, wriggling, almanac, kennel, banana, scabbard, nevertheless

Unit 5

1 delicate, decade, detergent, destroyed (devastated), detonate

2 despise-hate; definite-sure; desolate-lonely; delicate-fragile; detonate-ignite; devour-eat; deprive-withhold

3 desperation, devastation, delegation, deprivation, deletion, desolation, definition, determination, detonation, destitution

4 delicately, desperately, delightfully, definitely, desirably, deliberately

5 destroys, destroying, destroyed; detonates, detonating, detonated; despises, despising, despised; devours, devouring, devoured; devastates, devastating, devastated

6 delay – postpone; deflect – divert; decree – order; defend – protect; decrease – reduce; defeat – conquer; defrost – thaw; dejected – unhappy; defy – oppose; demure – shy

7 Birthdays are a time for **celebration** and **reflection**. A time to look back over the **past months** of your life; to ponder the ups and downs, and the highs and lows of your year. What **knowledge** have you gained? What new skills? Have you taken up a new **hobby** or learned to play a **musical instrument**? What people have left your life, or **entered** it for the first time? There is so much to look back on — maybe with pride, maybe with sadness. What have you **achieved** both inside your school and outside, and what are your goals for the next year of your life?

8 Writing activity

Unit 6

1 translated, interrupted, interval, transported, transforms

2 intervenes, intervening, intervened; intercepts, intercepting, intercepted; interferes, interfering, interfered; transmits, transmitting, transmitted; translates, translating, translated; transfers, transferring, transferred

3 interaction, interruption, intersection, interjection, intervention, transaction, transformation, translation, transportation, transition

4 ship, raft, yacht, canoe, dinghy, catamaran, kayak

5 interstate, transplant, transfixed, interspersed, transfusion

6 interact, react, exact, transact; intercept, except, concept, percept; interject, reject, project, inject

7 Writing activity

8 intercede: to act on behalf of someone who is in trouble; interlace: to weave in and out of each other; intertwine; interchange: to exchange places; trade; switch; swap; interlude: short break in proceedings; recess; music playing during an interval; intercom: system for sending messages within a building; intercommunication; interplay: the way two (or more) things have an effect on each other

9 intermediate: coming between two things in time, place or stage of life; midway; intermittent: happening now and again; stopping and starting; irregular; interrogative: forming a question; international: between or among countries across the world; transitory: brief; lasting for a short time; transient; transformer: electrical device used for changing one voltage to another; transcend: to go above and beyond expectation; surpass; exceed

Unit 7

1 computer, completely, confirmed, constructing, confiscated

2 comply-obey; compulsory-required; consider-ponder; confiscate-seize; compute-calculate; convalesce-recuperate; conscious-aware

3 completes, completing, completed; complies, complying, complied; congratulates, congratulating, congratulated; conveys, conveying, conveyed; communicates, communicating, communicated; conserves, conserving, conserved

4 Writing activity

5 complexion, conservation, conference, commendation, convalescence, congratulations

6 commendable, conditional, concealable, continual, constructive, comparable, considerable, consolable

7 Writing activity

Unit 8

1 permitted, impeding, Centipedes (Millipedes), committed, pedalling

2 permit, permitting, permitted; remit, remitting, remitted; transmit, transmitting, transmitted; submit, submitting, submitted; emit, emitting, emitted, commit, committing, committed

3 commission, permission, transmission, remission, submission, emission

4 pedal-lever; permit-allow; impede-block; expedition-journey; pedestrian-walker; intermission-interval; remiss-careless

5 missiles, remiss, permission, pedestal, pedestrian, stampede

6 impediment: an obstruction to doing something; obstacle; barrier; handicap; pedometer: a device for recording the number of steps a person takes; dismissive: showing something as unworthy of notice; scornful; offhand; biped: a two-legged creature; quadruped: a four-footed animal; emissary: a government representative sent on a special mission; diplomat; expedite: to make something happen sooner or more quickly; speed up

7 Examples: 4-letter: aids, airs, anti, ants, apes, area, arts, dare, dart, dead, dear, deed, deep, deer, dies, diet, dine, dire, drat, drip, earn, ears, east, eats, edit, ends, idea, nape, near, neat, need, nerd, nest, paid, pain, pair, pane, pant, pare, part, past, pear, peas, peat, peer, pest, pied, pies, pine, pint, raid, rain, rant, rasp, rate, read, reap, rent, rest, ride, rind, rise, said, sand, sane, sate, seat, seed, seen, seep, send, sent, side, site, spat, spit, star, step, tape, tear, teas, teen, tide, ties, tire, trap, tree, trip

5-letter: adept, arise, diner, drain, drape, earnt, Easter, enter, neater, paint, pants, parts, paste, pride, pried, pries, print, prise, raise, rinse, risen, saint, spate, spear, spend, spent, spite, stain, stare, stead, steep, steer, strap, strip, tease, train, tread, tried, tries

5+-letter: ardent, dearest, earnest, nastier, neater, nested, panted, pester, pirate, praise, rinsed, speared, strain, stride, strident, stripe

Term 1 review

1 centipede/millipede, wrestling, pedestrian (crossing), gnome, pedestal

2 dismisses, dismissing, dismissed; commits, committing, committed; deprives, depriving, deprived; complies, complying, complied; disfigures, disfiguring, disfigured; pedals, pedalling, pedalled

3 dislocate, uncomplicated, impatient, incomplete, discredit, indelicate, uninterrupted, unconscious, inconsiderate, disembark, indefinite, unconditional

4 imitation, observation, permission, interference, obstruction, convalescence, indulgence, perspiration, immunisation, transmission, transference, commendation

5 individual, discuss, persuade, construct, inferior, inhale, writhe, detergent, imitate, wreath

6 transparent, missile, disguise, intersection, compulsory, obstacle (obstruction), interrupt (interject), conscious, pedestal, intermittent

7 persuade, destroy, descend, perform, devour, personnel, despise, perfume, perspire, describe

8 The first **modern** Olympic Games were held in Greece in 1896. At that time, nine sports were contested. Over the **past** one hundred years, many sports have been added and **removed** from the Olympic program. Only five sports have been contested at **every** summer Olympic Games: swimming, athletics, cycling, **gymnastics** and fencing.

Australia's Olympic team has grown from one **competitor** in 1904 to 422 in Rio de Janeiro in 2016 with representatives in all 26 sports.

Friendly rivalry has long existed between Australia and the USA in the swimmming pool. Ian Thorpe is Australia's most prolific medalist, having won a total of five gold medals, three **silver** and one bronze in two Olympic Games.

Michael Phelps of the USA is **acclaimed** as the greatest swimmer of all time. He has won a **staggering** 23 gold medals in four Olympic Games.

Unit 9

1 excavating, apologised, navigator, investigating, exercising

2 organise-arrange; advertise-promote; irritate-annoy; estimate-guess; analyse-examine; nominate-name; minimise-lessen

3 operation, criticism, navigation, estimation, excavation, organisation, population, terrorism, nomination, irritation

4 publicise: to make something widely known to people; maximise: to make as large or great as possible; make the best use of; idolise: to admire greatly; adore; hero-worship; penalise: to punish; put at a disadvantage; improvise: to create and perform something without preparation; realise: to become fully aware of something; clearly understand; finalise: to bring to an end; conclude; complete; finish up

5 recognise, apologise, advertise, terrorise, irritate, analyse, summarise, investigate, energise, publicise

6 pop u la tion; op er a tion; ex er cise; ad vert ise ment; a pol o gy

7 vacate – leave somewhere; exit or depart from; hesitate – pause when unsure; hang back; vibrate – quiver, shake or tremble; radiate – send out rays of light or heat; activate – put something into action; start up; graduate – successfully complete a course of study; duplicate: make an exact copy of; inflate: fill with air or gas; pump up

8 vacation, hesitation, vibration, radiation, activation, graduation, duplication, inflation

9 swimming, gymnastics, athletics, rowing, cycling, archery

Unit 10

1 piano, avocado, tomato, potato, volcano

2 solos, cellos, photos, radios, silos, pianos, studios, avocados; heroes, potatoes, cargoes, volcanoes, echoes, tomatoes, tornadoes, mosquitoes

3 expo: international exhibition; calico: cotton cloth; polo: game played on horseback; banjo: round, stringed instrument; tempo: rhythm or beat in music; poncho: cloak with a hole for the head; dingo: Australian wild dog; gelato: Italian ice-cream; pesto: sauce served with pasta

4 speedo: car's odometer to measure speed; gusto: with enthusiasm and enjoyment; combo: a combination of different foods; pronto: quickly; promptly; arvo: the afternoon; cheerio: good-bye; little red sausage; aggro: aggressive behaviour; kilo: a kilogram

5 The cello is a member of the string family of **musical** instruments. Like the violin, it has four strings stretched over a bridge anchored at the top by four pegs. The player turns these pegs to **loosen** or tighten the strings to tune their instrument so that the sounds blend **together** and are **pleasant** to the ear. Like the violin, the cello is played by moving a bow across the strings. Sometimes the strings are **plucked** by the player for a **particular** effect.

The cello has a deep, rich tonal **quality** and is often played as a solo instrument **accompanied** by piano. The cello also forms part of a trio, quartet or full orchestra.

6 Writing activity

For the music buffs: soprano: highest female singing voice; alto: second-highest female singing voice; falsetto: singing higher than the usual vocal range; crescendo: becoming louder: decrescendo: becoming softer; pianissimo: very soft; moderato: of moderate speed; presto: very fast; lento: slow; concerto: music for solo instrument/s with orchestra; oratorio: a large sacred work for soloists, choir and orchestra

Unit 11

1 verify-confirm; mystify-bewilder; classify-sort; notify-tell; intensify-increase; defy-oppose; identify-recognise

2 classifies, classifying, classified, classifier; qualifies, qualifying, qualified, qualifier; magnifies, magnifying, magnified, magnifier; modifies, modifying, modified, modifier; pacifies, pacifying, pacified, pacifier

3 clarification, clarity; identification, identity; intensification; intensity; qualification, quality

4 signify, significance, significant; defy, defiant, defiance; testify, testimony, testament, testifier; simplify, simplicity, simply; justify, justice, justification, justifiable; magnify, magnification, magnificent

5 qualities, terrifying, identified, defiantly, mystified

6 rectify: to put right; repair; fix up; remedy; certify: to confirm something; guarantee; verify; endorse; specify: to state something clearly and precisely; detail; define; itemise; solidify: to become hard; set; freeze; thicken;

stiffen; purify: to make pure; cleanse; decontaminate; falsify: to make something incorrect, especially to deceive someone; to fake; petrify: to make someone so frightened they cannot move

7 Writing activity

8 Examples: 4-letter words: aims, airs, ants, arms, arts, earn, ears, east, elms, emit, isle, item, lair, lame, lane, last, late, lean, lens, lent, lies, line, lint, list, lure, mail, main, male, malt, mane, mare, mast, mate, meal, mean, meat, melt, mile, mine, mint, mire, mist, mite, mule, muse, must, mute, nail, name, neat, nest, nine, nuts, rail, rain, rant, rate, real, ream, rein, rent, rest, rile, rise, ruin, rule, runt, ruse, rust, sail, sale, salt, same, seal, seam, seat, sent, silt, sire, site, slam, slat, slim, slit, slum, slur, stir, stun, suit, tail, tale, tame, team, tear, tent, test, ties, tile, tilt, time, tine, tins, tint, tire, tram, true, tune

5-letter words: alter, amuse, earnt, lairs, later, leant, learn, least, liars, meant, merit, miner, miser, mural, raise, ruins, saint, slain, slant, slate, slime, smile, smite, snail, stale, stare, steal, steam, stile, stilt, stint, strum, stunt, treat, trust

5+letter words: entail, insert, instant, island, lament, master, menial, mental, mister, muster, remain, rental, retail, silent, stamen, stilts, strain, strait, stream, talent, tinsel, tunnel

Unit 12

1 arranging, terraces, digitally, centuries, celebrating, urgently

2 agendas, engines, policies, successes, cereals

3 region-area; legend-tale; accident-mishap; cereal-grain; engine-motor; emerge-appear; policy-plan

4 arranges, arranging, arranged; obliges, obliging, obliged; celebrates, celebrating, celebrated; polices, policing, policed; emerges, emerging, emerged

5 cent: a coin equal to one hundredth of a dollar; centenary: the hundredth anniversary of an event; centurion: an officer commanding one hundred men; percentage: a number out of one hundred; %; centipede: an insect with many pairs of feet; bicentennial: celebrating two hundred years; centigrade: a heat scale from 0 to 100 degrees; centenarian: a person of one hundred years or more

6 regional, successful, celebratory, emergent, legendary, incidental, central, political

7 correct answers: incidents, urgent, century, terrain, policy

8 coincidence: the surprising occurrence of two things at the same time; emergency: an unexpected, often serious, situation requiring immediate action; cylinder: a tube-shaped object with circular ends; generation: people born and living at the same time, e.g. 1990s; decipher: to solve a puzzle; work out; break the code; cinnamon: a spice obtained from the bark of a tree and used in cooking

Unit 13

1 governors, tenors, scholars, sculptors, liars

2 vendor-seller; tenor-singer; regular-usual; similar-alike; scholar-student; solicitor-lawyer; spectacular-eye-catching

3 regularly, similarly, popularly, scholarly, spectacularly, peculiarly

4 sculpt, sculpture; govern, government; survive, survival; instruct, instruction; direct, directory

5 tenor, liar, binoculars, regular(ly), singular (single), commentator, nectar, sculptor, author

6 jacaranda, tepee, salary, remember, placard, September, drama, seventeen, element, Mississippi

7 Writing activity

Unit 14

1 bicycles, microphones, monolgues, microscopes, monopolies

2 attractively, expressively, impressively, productively, sensitively, attentively, pensively; attractiveness, expressiveness, impressiveness, productivity (productiveness), sensitivity (sensitiveness), attentiveness, pensiveness

3 pensive-thoughtful; imperative-crucial; expensive-dear; bicycle-bike; intensive-thorough; selective-choosy; active-busy

4 unattractive, inexpensive, unproductive, insensitive, unimpressive, inactive

5 two, three, one, two, three, two, three, three, One, three, one

6 The Eurovision Song Contest is an **annual** international TV song contest held particularly among members of the European Broadcasting Union. Singers from participating countries receive votes from both a panel of judges and the **general** viewing public. It is a glittering, **glamorous** occasion with a large live **audience** and millions of viewers across the world.

In 2015, Australia was invited to participate in the contest for the first time. Dami Im was chosen to sing for Australia in 2016 following her **success** in the TV music **competition** *The X Factor*. Dami made it through the semi-finals to reach the Grand Final, where she **received** a standing ovation for a **spectacular** rendition of her song, 'Sound of Silence', which was **specially** written for the contest. When all the votes were counted, Dami was awarded second place, bringing her worldwide **recognition**.

7 Writing activity

Unit 15

1 election, extinguisher, expiry, elevation, extravagance, extinction

2 excel, exhaust, example, excited, explore, extend; equip, evolve, eclipse, evacuate, eject, equality

3 extinct-long-dead; exclude-omit; elapse-pass; eliminate-discard; eligible-qualified; expire-die; elevate-raise

4 elastic, elaborate, extravagant, eliminated, elements, experience, elevator

5 exhibition, exclusion, elimination, evasion, examination, exhalation, elevation, evacuation

6 explicit, elapsed, inspired, included, distinguish

7 exposition: 1. large public show of arts or trade goods; 2. a detailed explanation; exquisite: gorgeous; stunning; delicate; beautiful; exterminate: to get rid of something by destroying it; exuberant: full of energy and excitement; in high spirits; cheerful; excursion: a short trip, usually for a specific reason; exemplary: perfect; ideal; being a good example to follow

8 violet, circular, surfboard, carousel, fragile, costumes, doubling, comedian, medium, suspension

Unit 16

1 endangered, enquiries, entirely, entangled, ensuing, entitled

2 enchant-delight; envisage-imagine; endeavour-try; ensue-follow; entreat-beg; endorse-support; entire-whole

3 enrol, enfold, engrave, engage, enlist, enable, encode, encourage; tighten, weaken, golden, shorten, smarten, olden, quicken, deaden

4 enchants, enchanting, enchanted; entices, enticing, enticed; endorses, endorsing, endorsed; endures, enduring, endured; enthrals, enthralling, enthralled

5 entertainment, enlargement, endorsement, entitlement, enforcement, enchantment, enticement, entanglement

6 Writing activity

Term 2 review

1 piano, binoculars, avocado, bicycle, volcano, cello, policeman, tomato, tornado, radio

2 potatoes, policies, exercises, chemists, apologies, cargoes, successes, energies, studios, centuries, terraces, heroes

3 recognising, enthralling, terrifying, separating, enticing; signified, expelled, censored, enquired, defied; operator, classifier, navigator, elevator, advertiser

4 solicitor, century, author, dollar, similar, solo, tornado, elastic, engine, exclude, photo, enquire

5 extravagance, exclusion, advertisement, extinction, endurance, magnification, arrangement, defiance, enforcement, organisation

6 insure, extinct, sensor, biennial, enforce, extinguish

7 silo, centre, liar, Endeavour, tenor, sculptor, magnifying, photo, identity, accident

8 disorganised, unsuccessful, disenchanted, unimpressed, unqualified (disqualified), inactive, inexperienced, dissimilar, unverified

9 nectar, excavate, bicycle, govern, election, criticise, centipede, microwave, volcano, monologue

Unit 17

1 retrieve, recommend, relative, resemble, register, remedy

2 recollect-remember; remedy-cure; restrict-limit; recuperate-recover; reluctant-unwilling; renovate-restore; remunerate-pay

3 return, retire, retrace, reverse, revise, review, relay, relax, relent, remote, remorse, remind

4 restriction, recuperation, remuneration, relation, recollection, recommendation, renovation, regulation

5 retrieving, renovating, resembling, replenishing, reminiscing; restricted, recuperated, recollected, resonated, regulated

6 rehearsal: a private practice session before performing in public; reinforce: to make stronger by adding something extra; refund: to pay back (money); revolution: 1 huge change 2 overthrow of government 3 one turn on an axis; refectory: dining hall in a university; refugee: someone who escapes to another country for safety

7 Writing activity

8 Examples: 4-letter words: airs, amen, ants, arts, earn, ears, east, eats, emit, eras, even, ever, evil, iron, isle, item, lair, lame, lane, last, late, lean, lent, lies, lime, line, lint, lion, list, loam, loan, lone, lost, love, mail, main, male, malt, mane, mare, mast, mate, meal, mean, meat, meet, melt, mile, mine, mint, mire, mist, moan, more, most, move, nail, name, near, neat, nest, nine, norm, note, oats, oils, omen, oval, oven, over, rail, rain, rant, rate, rave, real, ream, rear, reel, rent, rest, riot, roam, roan, rove, sail, sale, salt, same, sane, sate, save, seal, seam, seat, seem, seen, sent, silt, site, sore, sort, star, tail, tale, teal, team, tear, teem, tens, tent, term, test, tier, tile, tilt, time, tine, tire, toil, tone, torn, tram, trim, vain, vale, vane, vast, veal, veer, veil, vein, vent, vest, vile, vine, vote

5-letter words: aisle, alert, alive, alone, avert, email, enter, event, inner, irate, leant, learn, least, liner, manor, meant, metal, naval, navel, never, rains, raven, reins, reset, revel, rinse, river, rivet, saint, satin, serve, slant, slate, slave, sleet, slime, smile, smite, smote, snail, snort, stain, stale, stare, start, state, stave, steal, steam, steel, stern, stile, stilt, stole, stone, store, storm, stove, taint, tease, toast, total, trail, train, viola, vital, voter

5+letter words: antler, artist, attire, enlist, entail, entire, environs, innermost, invent, inventor, invite, lament, learnt, manner, marine, mariner, master, mental, mettle, mister, nettle, nostril, relate, relent, remain, remove, renovate, rental, resale, restore, retail, reveal, revolt, roster, sailor, salmon, sermon, servant, servile, settle, stamen, strain, stream, street, strive, tailor, talent, toilet, vermin, violent, violin, vitamin

Unit 18

1 subtraction, affection, invention, attraction, regulation, deduction, direction, perfection, rejection, exhibition, extraction, correction, distraction, injection, prevention, relation, projection, reduction

2 decorative, inclusive, explosive, conclusive, decisive, instructive, exclusive, impressive, attractive, expressive

3 include, exclude, conclude, erode, intrude, collide, divide, decide, explode, invade

4 coll is ion, dec or a tions, in struc tions, cap tion, re duc tion, res o lu tions

5 consideration, obligation, perspiration, immunisation, sensation, conservation, embarkation, confirmation, observation, transportation

6 instructional, exceptional, emotional, sensational, provisional

Unit 19

1 proclaimed, precisely, providing, precariously, prohibited

2 predicting, predicted, predictor; processing, processed, processor; propelling, propelled, propeller; protecting, protected, protector; providing, provided, provider

3 propel-push; proficient-skilled; predict-forecast; precise-exact; prohibit-ban; protect-defend; precarious-unsafe

4 prefer, pretend, predominate, prevent, prefix, preserve, precaution, predate, prefabricate, present, prehistoric, pretext; prolong, procure, profile, program, propose, provision, proceed, profess, profound, pronoun, proportion, protest

5 Writing activity
6 1 inhibit, 2 provoke, 3 divide, 4 prescribe, 5 proclaim, 6 contradict
7 preview, progress, propel, recede, conserve
8 protect, detect; previous, devious; preserve, deserve; process, recess; precise, concise

Unit 20

1 preceding, conducts, receding, deducted, accesses (accessed), inducted
2 proceed-continue; educate-teach; succeed-accomplish; induce-persuade; reduce-decrease; excess-surplus; produce-grow
3 reduces, reducing, reduced; processes, processing, processed; conducts, conducting, conducted; educates, educating, educated; recedes, receding, receded, deducts, deducting, deducted
4 deduction, production, induction, procession, reduction, introduction, education, succession
5 successful, excessive, educational, concessional, successive, productive, accessible, procedural
6 Writing activity
7 conductor, producer, educator, processor, successor
8 successful, procession, excessive, conduct, reduced, productive

Unit 21

1 personal, medical, Feral, federal, aboriginal, several
2 nature, medic, nation, origin, aborigine, person, trivia, grade
3 frugal-thrifty; actual-real; feral-wild; several-some; trivial-minor; rural-country; integral-necessary
4 personally, medically, naturally, frugally, actually, originally, gradually, manually, federally, centrally, nationally, casually
5 Writing activity
6 Writing activity
7 personality, originality, nationality, vitality, punctuality, individuality, locality, brutality
8 Writing activity
9 Australia is a **vast** island continent and home to about 25 million people. With an area of 7.6 million square **kilometres**, Australia is a land of great contrasts, from its dry central **plains**, to its wet **tropical** rainforests, to its cool southern climes where snow falls in parts of Victoria and Tasmania. The Great **Dividing** Range extends along the **eastern** coastline from north Queensland to central Victoria. To its east lie **fertile** plains and long stretches of golden, sandy beaches. Australia has some of the world's most diverse natural environments, **spectacular** scenery and an abundance of unique wildlife. There are over 500 **national** parks to delight visitors and 19 World Heritage-listed sites, both natural, such as Uluru and the Great Barrier Reef, and man-made, such as the Sydney **Opera** House.

Unit 22

1 pyramid, gymnasium, ferry, canary, pyjamas, physical
2 pyramids, gymnast, cymbals, canary, pyjamas
3 mysteries, fallacies, pulleys, libraries, countries, monkeys, industries, trolleys, valleys, lullabies, journeys, melodies
4 motley-assorted; ordinary-normal; fallacy-untruth; cylinder-tube; temporary-short-term; mutiny-revolt; gaudy-showy
5 mutinous, mysterious, industrious, temporarily, physically, ordinarily
6 mystify: to bewilder or confuse; perplex; physics: the field of science that studies matter and energy; python: a large, non-venomous snake that crushes its prey; physique: the shape of someone's body; pylon: a tall tower carrying electric or telephone wires; cygnet: a young swan
7 temporary, illustrate, cappuccino, solitude, barrier, influenza, spherical, surprise, trousers, banquet

Unit 23

1 hyphens, syringes, hydrants, symphonies, systems, hyenas, liquids, symbols, symptoms
2 hyena, Synthetic, symphony, hyphen, hybrid
3 symphonic, hygienic, symbolic, hypnotic, systematic, sympathetic
4 hydrogen, syrup, symptom, hydrant, symbol, syringe
5 music, happy, love, at (email address), poison, correct
6 Writing activity
7 baseball, hockey, tennis, basketball, squash, cricket

Unit 24

1 absently, accounts, accelerated, accomplishing, accepted
2 accurate-correct; abduct-kidnap; absurd-silly; accomplish-achieve; abrupt-sudden; abundant-plentiful; abbreviate-shorten
3 accurately, absolutely, abruptly, abundantly, absently, accidentally; abduction, accession, abbreviation, acceleration, accumulation, accommodation
4 accepted, accommodation, absent, absorbent, abrupt
5 Writing activity
6 absorb, account, accomplish, absolute, accept, accurate, accident, abrupt: GUM BOOTS
7 abseiling: sport of lowering oneself down a cliff using ropes; absentee: a person who is not present; who does not 'show up'; accountant: a person whose job is to examine the financial records of a business; accuse: to blame someone for some wrongdoing; accentuate: to make something stand out; highlight; underline

Term 3 review

1 pyramids, hydrant, cymbals, cylinder, pyjamas
2 successes, industries, symptoms, mysteries, remedies, decisions, processes, symphonies, emotions, accounts, canaries, fallacies
3 processes, processing, processed; regulates, regulating, regulated; absorbs, absorbing, absorbed; reduces, reducing, reduced; propels, propelling, propelled; accompanies, accompanying, accompanied; prohibits, prohibiting, prohibited; reminisces, reminiscing, reminisced
4 Writing activity (word knowledge)
5 educator, decorator, producer, refrigerator, regulator, conductor, provider, propeller, processor, renovator, instructor, protector

6 accurate, absent, ordinary, feral, lullaby, symbol, abduct, resemble, accelerate, remedy, journey, punctual

7 entertainment, endurance, recommendation, collision, entitlement, resemblance, reduction, conclusion, enchantment, acceptance, precision, accompaniment

8 ferry, gymnasts, hyena, pollution, abbreviation, library, hydrogen, conductor, abdomen, liquids

Unit 25

1 angry-furious; tasty-delicious; polite-courteous; beautiful-gorgeous; huge-enormous; wealthy-prosperous; valuable-precious; roomy-spacious; hungry-ravenous

2 arduous-difficult; obvious-clear; various-assorted; pompous-haughty; devious-dishonest; curious-inquisitive; gracious-polite

3 curiously, graciously, dangerously, furiously, pompously, generously, obviously, enormously, deliciously, seriously

4 fury, grace, danger, disaster, glamour, space, prosper, glory

5 Examples: delicious food, arduous task, enormous elephant, precious jewels, courteous gentleman, curious children

6 joyous (joyful), adventurous, plentiful, colourful, courageous, mischievous, famous, hazardous, fearful, doubtful, envious, victorious

7 prosperous-prosperity; anxious-anxiety; courteous-courtesy; delicious-delicacy; various-variety; gracious-graciousness; studious-study; generous-generosity; enormous-enormity

8 Over four hundred years ago, a German astronomer named Johann Kepler exclaimed, "We must **build** a ship to sail the oceans of space in the universe!" This became a **reality** in the 20th century with the landing of man on the moon and the **launching** of many space probes to **unravel** the secrets of the stars. Using the **powerful** Kepler telescope NASA continues to probe the sky for signs of life on distant **planets**. In July 2016, an **international** team of scientists **announced** that they had discovered a four-planet solar system, 181 light-years away, which may support life.

9 Examples: 4-letter: ants, arts, dare, date, dear, dent, done, dose, dote, dour, dove, duet, dune, dust, earn, east, eats, ends, nave, near, neat, node, nose, note, nuts, oars, oats, ours, oven, over, rant, rave, read, rend, rent, rest, roan, rose, rout, rove, runt, rust, sand, sane, sate, save, seat, sent, soar, sore, sort, sour, star, sure, tear, tend, tone, tons, trod, tune, utes, vane, vase, vast, vent, vest, vote

5-letter: adore, avert, drone, drove, ovens, overt, raven, roast, round, route, snore, stand, stare, stead, stone, store, stove, tours, trade, tread, trove, under

5+letter: advent, arduous, detour, devour, servant, soared, soured, strode, strove, sunder, toured, tundra, vendor

Unit 26

1 dial, crocodile, diagnose, diamond, mobile, diameter

2 dialogue-talk; agile-nimble; futile-useless; juvenile-teenager; diagram-drawing; docile-gentle; hostile-unfriendly

3 fertility, futility, hostility, sterility, agility, docility, mobility, versatility

4 fertilise, fertiliser, fertilisation, fertility; sterilise, steriliser, sterilisation, sterility; mobilise, mobilisation, mobility

5 diagnosing, diagonally, diamonds, docilely, Crocodiles

6 Writing activity

7 mistake, communicate, abdomen, radius, ignore, comedian, gadgets, enthralling, chronicle, tulips

Unit 27

1 legible, audible, manageable, combustible, infallible, intelligible, invisible, invincible

2 durable-lasting; plausible-believable; valuable-precious; hospitable-friendly; fashionable-stylish; admissible-acceptable; tolerable-bearable

3 durability, infallibility, responsibility, capability, reliability, probability, legibility, invisibility, flexibility, respectability

4 eligible, accessible, inflatable, achievable, considerable

5 undesirable, uninhabitable, improbable, inaudible, unreasonable, impossible, invisible, implausible, intolerable, unmanageable, unintelligible, inhospitable

6 plausible, legibly, invisible, audible, hospitable

Unit 28

1 Exuding, demurely, concluding, assured, obscuring

2 conclude-end; pasture-grass; altitude-height; obscure-hide/vague; aptitude-ability; mature-ripe; fortitude-strength

3 assuring, assured; obscuring, obscured; enduring, endured; exuding, exuded; intruding, intruded

4 Writing activity

5 assurance, conclusion, maturity (maturation), invasion, exclusion, intrusion, obscurity, endurance, protrusion, security

6 posture, assure, intrude, excluded, aptitude

7 longitude: distance east or west of Greenwich measured in degrees; temperamental: someone moody, excitable, unpredictable, hot-headed; interlude: a short period of time or rest; interval; recess; signature: name written in a distinctive way as a form of ID; brochure: a book/pamphlet containing information about a product/service; magnitude: the size or extent of something; greatness; importance; caricature: a picture exaggerating certain features to create a comic effect; horticulture: the growing of plants for their fruit, vegetables and flowers

8 temperature, gratitude, pressure, attitude, pasture, altitude

Unit 29

1 mosquito, mosque, sapphire, pharmacy, bouquet

2 typhoons, mosquitoes, orphans, graphs, sapphires, dolphins, sequences, banquets

3 typhoon-hurricane; antique-ancient; pharaoh-king; tranquil-calm; phoney-fake; conquer-defeat; banquet-feast

4 orphanage, conqueror, biography, antiquity, pharmacist, tranquillity, tranquillise, graphic

5 consequence: result of an action, usually unpleasant; phenomenon: unusual occurrence not always understood; photograph: image taken by a camera; quintuplets: five babies born at the same time; equestrian: horse rider (noun); related to horse riding (adjective); emphasis: stress/importance placed on something

6 The great steed snorted and **pawed** the ground, held in check by its rider Sir Ralph de Berg, a brave and **intrepid** knight. The iron gate rattled upward, and horse and rider burst across the **lowered** drawbridge at break-neck speed. Sir Ralph had been dispatched on a **desperate** quest to rescue the Lady Catherine, who had been **kidnapped** by enemies of the king during a daring night raid.

By nightfall, he had reached the outskirts of the enemy's camp and drew in the horse's **reins**. He tethered his trusty steed to a tree and crept soundlessly forward towards the **gathering** of tents. He caught a glimpse of the Lady Catherine, arms tied, as she was pushed **roughly** into a tent at the edge of the camp. Sir Ralph drew back into the shadows and circled his way around the camp until he was behind the Lady's tent…

7 Writing activity

Unit 30

1 pedestrian, politicians, commercial, optician, musicians

2 partial-partly; initial-beginning; crucial-important; official-formal; pedestrian-walker; special-extraordinary; guardian-protector

3 officially, partially, initially, crucially, socially, essentially, spatially, specially, commercially, racially

4 musical, technical, electrical, magical, optical, political, mathematical, clinical

5 soloist, electrician, doctor, comedian, cartoonist, musician, pianist, jogger, conductor, sculptor

6 finance, equator, colony, bacteria, face, picture, memory

7 Writing activity

Unit 31

1 obedient, magnificent; defendant, different, servants

2 evident-obvious; assistant-helper; confident-self-assured; despondent-sad; different-unalike; efficient-competent; insolent-rude

3 independently, obediently, evidently, insolently, frequently, confidently, magnificently, despondently, efficiently, pleasantly

4 contestants, pageant; disobedient, insolent; settlement, inhabitants; confident, efficient; different, accident; language, consonants

5 confidence, evidence, obedience, magnificence, insolence, dependence; assistance, attendance, dominance, relevance, brilliance, importance; despondency, dependency, efficiency, competency, frequency, decency; infancy, consultancy, expectancy, accountancy, hesitancy, vacancy

6 possessing, waddled, toaster, obstacle, monument, imposter, momentary, pincers, circus, ordinary

Unit 32

1 stylish, fashionable; famous, renowned; obedient, dutiful; wasteful, flamboyant; rude, cheeky; marvellous, wonderful

2 defence-protection; maintenance-upkeep; influence-effect; balance-steadiness; occurrence-happening; reference-mention; radiance-glow

3 occur, occurring, occurred; rely, relying, relied; confer, conferring, conferred; maintain, maintaining, maintained; refer, referring, referred

4 assurance, endurance, observance, guidance, performance, admittance, resemblance; dependence, obedience, interference, transference, reminiscence, emergence, precedence

5 reliant, reliance; compliant, compliance; existent, existence; ignorant, ignorance; dependent, dependence; defiant, defiance, referee, reference; excellent, excellence; persistent, persistence; important, importance

6 referendum: a public (yes/no) vote on a question of government or law; vigilance: a state of being alert and watchful; tolerance: the ability to accept opinions and beliefs that are different to your own; coincidence: things happening together by chance; alliance: an agreement to work together to achieve a result; negligence: failure to take proper care and attention

Term 4 review

1 mosquito, crocodile, diamond, ambulance, dolphin, pharaoh, bouquet, elephant

2 endures, enduring, endured; relies, relying, relied; concludes, concluding, concluded, occurs, occurring, occurred; excels, excelling, excelled

3 confident, hospital, exclude, possible, invincible

4 assistant, conquer, banquet, juvenile, curious, commercial, impudent, fertile, dial, physique, diagram, temperature

5 visible, audible, durable, fashionable, legible, valuable, combustible, hospitable

6 infertile, impossible, unconfident, intolerable, undesirable, inexperienced, unmanageable, immature, inefficient, improbable, unglamorous, unreasonable

7 collection, musician, maturity (maturation), exclusion, antiquity, speciality, conclusion, guardian, hostility, electricity (electrician)

8 consonants, different, obedient, dependent, servant, confident, frequent, recent

9 Applied word knowledge. A diary is a book for recording daily events. A dairy is a place on a farm where cows are milked.

5 Build nouns by adding suffixes.

Choose from -ance, -ment or -ion/-tion/-sion. ***(Apply any tips or rules.)***

extravagant	______________	magnify	______________
exclude	______________	arrange	______________
advertise	______________	defy	______________
extinct	______________	enforce	______________
endure	______________	organise	______________

6 Colour the correct word in the brackets.

Mr Reid will [ensure insure] his new car against accidents and theft.

Dinosaurs became [instinct extinct] millions of years ago.

A light [sensor censor] may be used in burglar alarms and garage door openers.

The piano competition is a [bilingual biennial] event.

The role of the police is to [endorse enforce] the laws of the state.

Firemen tried to [extinguish distinguish] the flames engulfing the shoe factory.

7 Answer the following questions.

What tall structure is used to store grain?	**s**______________
What word means the same as *middle* or *core*?	**c**______________
What is a person who tells untruths?	**l**______________
What was the name of Captain Cook's ship?	**E**______________
What is a high-pitched male singing voice?	**t**______________
Who would carve a statue?	**s**______________
What type of 'glass' makes things appear much larger?	**m**______________
What is an image recorded by a camera?	**p**______________
What does an ID card show proof of?	**i**______________
What is a mishap?	**a**______________

8 Write antonyms using prefixes. Choose from dis-, in- or un-.

______organised	______impressed	______experienced
______successful	______qualified	______similar
______enchanted	______active	______verified

9 Add the missing letters to mend the broken words. Use the clues to help you.

collected by bees	n __ __ t __ __	find fault with	cr __ t __ __ i __ __
dig a tunnel	ex __ __ v __ __ __	insect with many legs	c __ __ t __ p __ __ __
two-wheeled bike	bi __ __ __ __ __	type of oven	mi __ __ __ w __ v __
to rule	g __ v __ __ n	exploding mountain	v __ l __ __ n __
choice by voting	el __ __ __ __ __ n	speech by one person	m __ n __ l __ g __ __

Prefixes: re-

The **prefix** re- means 'again' or 'back' *(**rebuild** = build again; **repay** = pay back)*. **NOTE:** In the first part of the *See and Say* list, the **re-** is pronounced with a long vowel, e.g. ***rēstrict***. In the second part of the list, the **re-** is pronounced with a short vowel, e.g. ***rĕgulate***.

SEE & SAY

retrieve	religion	reluctant	recollect	register	remedy
reprieve	resemble	recuperate	recommend	relative	renovate
replenish	restrict	remunerate	regulate	reminisce	resonate

1 Choose a word from the *See and Say* list to complete these sentences.

Cory hit the ball over the fence and Kay has gone to **rē**_______________ it.

Health experts **rĕ**_______________ that we maintain a daily exercise routine.

My closest **rĕ**_______________ is Aunty Jean, and she lives in Tasmania.

Zoe has shaped the clay to **rē**_______________ a tree frog.

If you buy a dog, you will need to **rĕ**_______________ it with the council.

Chicken soup is a good old-fashioned **rĕ**_______________ for colds.

2 Colour the pairs of words that are synonyms. Use a different colour for each pair.

recollect	remedy	restrict	recuperate	reluctant	renovate	remunerate
recover	pay	unwilling	remember	cure	limit	restore

3 Build your word knowledge by adding the prefix re-.

_____turn	_____lay
_____tire	_____lax
_____trace	_____lent
_____verse	_____mote
_____vise	_____morse
_____view	_____mind

Read the words in each list two times. How many words can you remember? Write them in your notebook. Check and write your scores here.

....

4 Build nouns by adding the suffix -ion. *(Apply any rules and tips.)*

restrict	_______________	recollect	_______________
recuperate	_______________	recommend	_______________
remunerate	_______________	renovate	_______________
relate	_______________	regulate	_______________

WORD EXTRA recede refrigerate

TARGETING SPELLING 6 © PASCAL PRESS ISBN 9781925490244

UNIT 17

5 Write the present and past participles of these verbs.

Add -ing		Add -ed	
retrieve		restrict	
renovate		recuperate	
resemble		recollect	
replenish		resonate	
reminisce		regulate	

6 Say these words then match them to their meanings. Use a dictionary to help you.

reg ist rar	to pay back (money)
re hear sal	1. someone who keeps records 2. a doctor training to be a specialist
re in force	1. huge change 2. overthrow of government 3. one turn on an axis
re fund	someone who escapes to another country for safety
rev ō lū tion	to make stronger by adding something extra
re fec tor y	a private practice session before performing in public
ref ū gee	dining hall in a university

7 To reminisce is to recall past events in your life. Write a paragraph entitled *Reminiscences of My Childhood.*

8 Use the letters in this word to make new words. Write these words in columns in your notebook. Score your words and write your total score in the box.

environmentalist

Score 3 points for each 4-letter word.
Score 5 points for each 5-letter word.
Score 10 points for each 5+-letter word.

Suffixes: -ion

The Latin **suffix -ion** is attached to the end of a word to form a **noun**.
When added to a word ending in **t** or **te**, it becomes **-tion** (the **e** is dropped).
Examples: act, action; pollute, pollution

SEE & SAY

caution	pollution	instruction	inclusion	occasion	collision
caption	decoration	reduction	exclusion	decision	impression
commotion	demolition	resolution	explosion	division	conclusion

A Little Lesson in Latin

facio (factus) – *I do/make,* as in *factor, factory, defect*

habeo (habitus) – *I hold,* as in *habitable, inhabit*

rego (rectus) – *I rule,* as in *regal, region, regulate*

fero (latus) – *I carry/bear,* as in *fertile, refer, relative*

jacio (jactus) – *I throw,* as in *reject, project, object, subject*

traho (tractus) – *I draw,* as in *track, abstract, distract*

venio (ventus) – *I come,* as in *adventure, event, convenient*

duco (ductus) – *I lead,* as in *duke, conduct, reduce*

1 **Build nouns by adding -ion. Choose a partner to discuss the new words and their meanings. *(Note the e rule.)***

subtract________	exhibit________
affect________	extract________
invent________	correct________
attract________	distract________
regulate________	inject________
deduct________	prevent________
direct________	relate________
perfect________	project________
reject________	reduce________

When a noun ends in **-ion**, add **-s** to write it in its plural form. *Examples: captions, collisions*
NOTE: Not all nouns ending in **-ion** have a plural form. *Examples: pollution, commotion*
If used as the **subject** of a sentence, such words are followed by a *singular verb.*

2 **Change these nouns to adjectives by changing the suffix -ion to -ive.**

decoration ____________________	instruction ____________________
inclusion ____________________	exclusion ____________________
explosion ____________________	impression ____________________
conclusion ____________________	attraction ____________________
decision ____________________	expression ____________________

WORD EXTRA

emotion exception

TARGETING SPELLING 6 © PASCAL PRESS ISBN 9781925490244

TIP

Because of their Latin roots, for many words ending in **-ade**, **-ide**, **-ode** and **-ude** change the **de** to **s** before adding **-ion**.
The roots of the words *include*, *exclude* and *conclude* are the Latin ***claudo clausus***. Note how the spelling changes when the suffix is added.
Examples: inclusion, exclusion, conclusion
The root of *provide* is ***video visus***, so *provide* becomes *provision*.

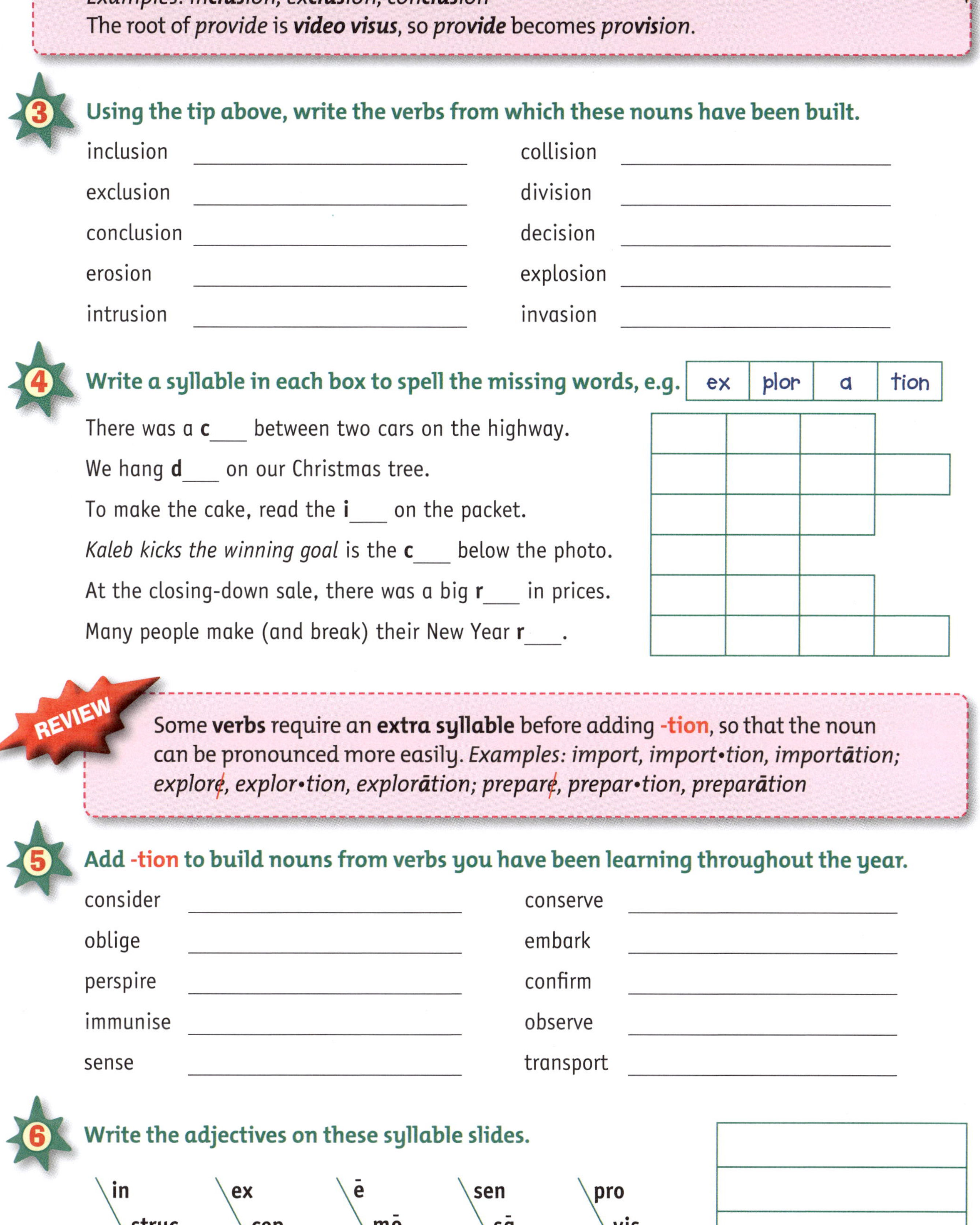

3 **Using the tip above, write the verbs from which these nouns have been built.**

inclusion	______	collision	______
exclusion	______	division	______
conclusion	______	decision	______
erosion	______	explosion	______
intrusion	______	invasion	______

4 **Write a syllable in each box to spell the missing words, e.g.**

ex	plor	a	tion

There was a **c**___ between two cars on the highway.
We hang **d**___ on our Christmas tree.
To make the cake, read the **i**___ on the packet.
Kaleb kicks the winning goal is the **c**___ below the photo.
At the closing-down sale, there was a big **r**___ in prices.
Many people make (and break) their New Year **r**___.

REVIEW

Some **verbs** require an **extra syllable** before adding **-tion**, so that the noun can be pronounced more easily. *Examples: import, import•tion, importātion; explore, explor•tion, explorātion; prepare, prepar•tion, preparātion*

5 **Add -tion to build nouns from verbs you have been learning throughout the year.**

consider	______	conserve	______
oblige	______	embark	______
perspire	______	confirm	______
immunise	______	observe	______
sense	______	transport	______

6 **Write the adjectives on these syllable slides.**

in **struc** **tion** **al**

ex **cep** **tion** **al**

ē **mō** **tion** **al**

sen **sā** **tion** **al**

pro **vis** **ion** **al**

TARGETING SPELLING 6 © PASCAL PRESS ISBN 9781925490244

Prefixes: pre-, pro-

The **prefix pre-** means 'before' or 'prior to'.
In Latin, ***servo*** = *I keep, so **pre**serve = to keep for a long time.*
The **prefix pro-** means 'for' or 'forward'.
In Latin, ***pello*** = *I drive, so **pro**pel = to drive forward.*

SEE & SAY

precede	predict	predicament	protect	provoke	proclaim
precise	prescribe	preliminary	process	provide	prohibit
preclude	precarious	previous	progress	propel	proficient

Add endings to the words in bold to complete the sentences.

proclaim After three gruelling events, our team was __________________ the winner.

precise Follow the instructions __________________ for a great result.

provide Con's dad is __________________ all our camping equipment.

precarious Joe was perched __________________ on the top of the ladder.

prohibit Smoking is __________________ in almost all public spaces.

Complete this table.

	Add -ing (present participle)	Add -ed (past participle)	Add -er or -or (to form nouns)
predict			
process			
propel			
protect			
provide			

Colour the pairs of words that are synonyms. Use a different colour for each pair.

propel	proficient	predict	precise	prohibit	protect	precarious
unsafe	ban	forecast	defend	push	skilled	exact

Don't confuse **precede** and **proceed**.
Precede means to go before. *Example: An anthem will **precede** the main game.*
Proceed means to go forward. *Example: The game will **proceed** despite the wet weather.*

WORD EXTRA

preserve propose

TARGETING SPELLING 6 © PASCAL PRESS ISBN 9781925490244

Build your word knowledge by adding the prefixes pre- and pro-. Check the meanings of any unfamiliar words in the dictionary.

Add pre-		Add pro-	
______fer	______caution	______long	______ceed
______tend	______date	______cure	______fess
______dominate	______fabricate	______file	______found
______vent	______sent	______gram	______noun
______fix	______historic	______pose	______portion
______serve	______text	______vision	______test

Write two sentences to show two different meanings for the words present and bear.

1 ____

____

2 ____

____

Colour the verb in each box that matches the numbered meanings below.

1. prohibit inhibit	2. invoke provoke	3. provide divide	4. describe prescribe	5. proclaim exclaim	6. predict contradict

1. to hold back; hinder; block; hamper
2. to make someone/something angry or annoyed
3. to split up or separate into parts; pull apart
4. to order a treatment to help someone get better
5. to make a public announcement
6. to say the opposite of; challenge; deny

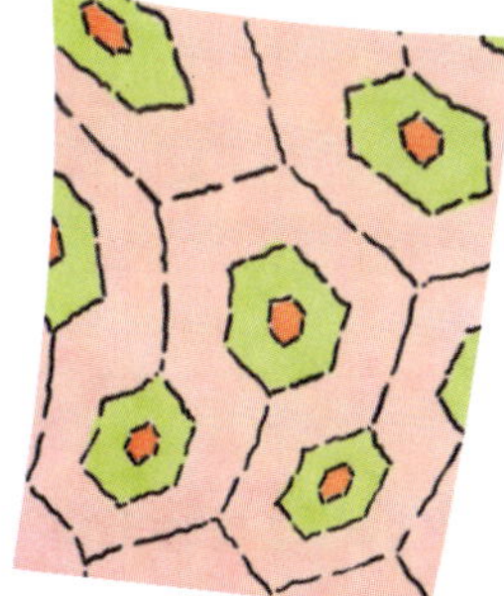

Colour the correct word in the brackets.

We saw a [preview interview] of the new animated movie *Pascale*.

Nadal's win in the semi-final saw him [process progress] to the final.

Wind in the sails helped [propel expel] the yacht into first position.

The rain has stopped and floodwaters have begun to [precede recede].

We need to [conserve preserve] our energy for the final climb to the summit.

8 Write the words by joining the two prefixes to each stem. Notice how prefixes change the meaning of words. Use a dictionary to check any unfamiliar words.

pro / de	pre / de	pre / de	pro / re	pre / con
tect	**vious**	**serve**	**cess**	**cise**
______	______	______	______	______
______	______	______	______	______

Latin Roots: duco ductus, cedo cessus

In Latin, ***in*** = *in* or *into;* ***duco ductus*** = *lead,*
so *induce* = *to lead into; de**duct*** = *to take from.*

Cedo cessus = *I go,*
so *ex**cess*** = *to go beyond; pro**ceed*** = *to go forward;*
*pre**cede*** = *to go before; re**cede*** = *to go back.*

SEE & SAY

conduct	product	induce	access	process	recede
deduct	produce	introduce	excess	proceed	precede
induct	reduce	educate	success	succeed	incessant

1 Add endings to the words in bold to complete the sentences.

precede In the hours ____________________ the storm, it was very hot and humid.

conduct Ms Edwards ____________________ the school choir.

recede The ____________________ tide left the beach scattered with broken shells.

deduct The cost of the broken bat was ____________________ from my pocket money.

access Cormac ____________________ the school grounds through a back gate.

induct Harry Lions will be ____________________ as school captain next Tuesday.

2 Colour the pairs of words that are synonyms. Use a different colour for each pair.

proceed	educate	succeed	induce	reduce	excess	produce
surplus	persuade	grow	teach	continue	accomplish	decrease

3 Complete this table of verbs.

	Add -s or -es	Add -ing	Add -ed
reduce			
process			
conduct			
educate			
recede			
deduct			

WORD EXTRA recess exceed

TARGETING SPELLING 6 © PASCAL PRESS ISBN 9781925490244

4 Build nouns by adding the suffix -ion.

deduct	________	reduce	________
product	________	introduce	________
induct	________	educate	________
process	________	success	________

5 Add these adjective-forming suffixes. Apply the e rule.

success + ful	________	success + ive	________
excess + ive	________	product + ive	________
education + al	________	access + ible	________
concession + al	________	procedure + al	________

6 Write sentences to show the difference in meaning between precede and proceed.

____

____

____

____

7 Colour the correct suffixes.

Vance Jonson is the conduct er/or of the symphony orchestra.

Simian Carter is a well-known movie produc er/or.

My niece Sarah is a nurse educat er/or.

Grace is using a word process er/or to write her assignment.

The Queen's success er/or is her son Charles.

8 Add the missing letters to mend the broken words.

Kieran's attempt to swim across the bay was **s** __ __ **cess** __ __ __.

A marching band led the **p** __ __ **cess** __ __ __ down the main street.

Accidents on the highway are often caused by **e** __ **cess** __ __ __ speed.

The teacher praised the students for their excellent **c** __ __ **duc** __.

The price of all items in the store has been **r** __ **duc** __ __ by 20 per cent.

The Downs is a very **p** __ __ **duc** __ __ __ __ wheat growing area.

How many words can you remember?

Go back and choose any *See and Say* list. Read through it twice, focusing on how the words look and sound. Write as many words as you can remember in your notebook. Check how many you have written correctly and enter your score here. ☐

Suffixes: -al

-al is an **adjective-forming suffix**. **-al**, **-el** and **-le** share the same sound **l** as in *camel*, *final* and *little*. Because words with these endings sound the same, you need to remember what the words *look* like.

SEE & SAY

central	frugal	medical	federal	manual	original
natural	personal	integral	feral	gradual	aboriginal
national	punctual	actual	trivial	several	individual

1 Choose a word from the *See and Say* list to complete the sentences.

A diary is a ____________________ record of the events that occur in your life.

I have an appointment with the doctor at the ____________________ centre.

____________________ cats are an increasing menace to native birds.

A ____________________ election was called to choose a new prime minister.

Oral storytelling is a rich part of the ____________________ culture.

The new block of apartments is ____________________ storeys high.

2 Write the nouns from which these adjectives have been built, *e.g. central, centre.*

natural	____________________	aboriginal	____________________
medical	____________________	personal	____________________
national	____________________	trivial	____________________
original	____________________	gradual	____________________

3 Colour the pairs of words that are synonyms. Use a different colour for each pair.

frugal	actual	feral	several	trivial	rural	integral
necessary	some	country	thrifty	wild	minor	real

4 Add -ly to these adjectives to form adverbs of manner.

personal ____________________	actual ____________________	federal ____________________
medical ____________________	original ____________________	central ____________________
natural ____________________	gradual ____________________	national ____________________
frugal ____________________	manual ____________________	casual ____________________

WORD EXTRA rural casual

TARGETING SPELLING 6 © PASCAL PRESS ISBN 9781925490244

5 Write sentences to show how the words manual and individual can be used 1. as an adjective and 2. as a noun.

1 ______________________

2 ______________________

1 ______________________

2 ______________________

6 Adjectives describe or classify nouns. Write a suitable noun beside each adjective.

feral ________	local ________	national ________
aboriginal ________	casual ________	personal ________
medical ________	rural ________	original ________
individual ________	several ________	central ________

7 Add the suffix -ity to build nouns from these adjectives.

personal ________	punctual ________
original ________	individual ________
national ________	local ________
vital ________	brutal ________

8 Choose two nouns from the list above and use them to write sentences.

____

____

____

____

9 Circle the spelling mistakes. Write them correctly in the box.

Australia is a varst island continent and home to about 25 million people. With an area of 7.6 million square kilometers, Australia is a land of great contrasts, from its dry central planes, to its wet tropicle rainforests, to its cool southern climes where snow falls in parts of Victoria and Tasmania. The Great Divideing Range extends along the easten coastline from north Queensland to central Victoria. To its east lie furtile plains and long stretches of golden, sandy beaches.

Australia has some of the world's most diverse natural environments, spectackula scenery and an abundance of unique wildlife. There are over 500 nationel parks to delight visitors and 19 World Heritage-listed sites, both natural, such as Uluru and the Great Barrier Reef, and man-made, such as the Sydney Opra House.

The letter y

The letter **y** is both a **consonant** (*yellow*, *canyon*) and a **vowel**.
Examples: an ī in *shy* and *cycle*; ĭ in *gym* and *cylinder*;
ē in *ferry* and *industry*.

SEE & SAY

mutiny	industry	ferry	cymbal	mystery	physical
motley	ordinary	fallacy	cylinder	pyramid	gymnasium
gaudy	temporary	canary	hysteria	pyjamas	lullaby

1 **Choose a word from the *See and Say* list to complete each sentence correctly. Add endings where necessary.**

Zoser was the first king of Egypt to build a ____________________.

Simone is training on the parallel bars in the ____________________.

We boarded a ____________________ to cross the Brisbane River.

A ____________________ is a small yellow singing bird often kept as a pet.

Cody is dressed in striped ____________________ and ready for bed.

We can maintain our ____________________ fitness through diet and exercise.

2 **Name the pictures.**

To write the plural form of **nouns** ending in **y**, follow these simple rules:

1. If the letter before the **y** is a vowel, just add **-s**. *Examples: boys, keys*
2. If the letter before the **y** is **not** a vowel, change **y** to **i** and add **-es**.
   Example: baby, babies

3 **Write these nouns in plural form.**

mystery ____________	country ____________	valley ____________
fallacy ____________	monkey ____________	lullaby ____________
pulley ____________	industry ____________	journey ____________
library ____________	trolley ____________	melody ____________

WORD EXTRA journey library

TARGETING SPELLING 6 © PASCAL PRESS ISBN 9781925490244

**Colour the pairs of words that are synonyms.
Use a different colour for each pair.**

motley	ordinary	fallacy	cylinder	temporary	mutiny	gaudy
revolt	showy	assorted	normal	untruth	tube	short-term

Don't confuse **cymbals** and **symbols**.
Cymbals are two brass plates struck together to make a musical sound.
Symbols are images that represent something that everyone can understand.
Examples: $ = money, ♥ = love

Build adjectives and adverbs. Apply the y rule. *(*Drop the y in this word.)*

mutiny + ous *	____________	temporary + ly	____________
mystery + ous	____________	physical + ly	____________
industry + ous	____________	ordinary + ly	____________

6 **Say these words then match them to their meanings. Use a dictionary to help you.**

myth ŏl ō gy	the field of science that studies matter and energy
mys ti fy	a large, non-venomous snake that crushes its prey
phys ics	a collection of ancient stories belonging to a particular culture
py thon	a tall tower carrying electric or telephone wires
phys ique	to bewilder or confuse; perplex
py lon	a young swan
cyg net	the shape of someone's body

Add vowels to mend the broken words. Use the clues to help you.
(Hint: All vowels in a word are different.)

T __ MP __ R __ RY	short term
__ LL __ STR __ T __	to draw pictures
C __ PP __ CC __ N __	coffee with frothy milk added
S __ L __ T __ D __	state of being alone/solitary
B __ RR __ __ R	an obstacle; something barring the way
__ NFL __ __ NZ __	infection causing fever, aches and pains
SPH __ R __ C __ L	shaped like a sphere or globe
S __ RPR __ S __	to startle; something unexpected
TR __ __ S __ RS	article of clothing; pants; jeans
B __ NQ __ __ T	large feast

Letter Teams: hy, sy

Many words beginning with **hy** and **sy** originate from the ancient language of Greek.

Hudor = *water*. From this root come the words *hydrant*, *hydrogen* and *hydroponics*.

Phone = *sound*. From this root come the words *symphony*, *phonics* and *cacophony (bad sound)*.

Hyper *(over)* and ***hypo*** *(under)* are Greek prefixes.
Derma = *skin*, so ***hypodermic*** = *under the skin*

SEE & SAY

hyena	hybrid	hydrant	syrup	symbol	symphony
hygiene	hyphen	hydroponic	syringe	symptom	synopsis
hype	hydrogen	hypodermic	system	sympathy	synthetic

1 Write these nouns in plural form.

hyphen	______	symphony	______	liquid	______
syringe	______	system	______	symbol	______
hydrant	______	hyena	______	symptom	______

2 Choose a word from the *See and Say* list to complete each sentence correctly. Add endings where necessary.

A ______________ is an African dog-like animal that scavenges and hunts for food.

______________ materials are often used in clothing instead of natural fibres.

The orchestra will play a ______________ composed by J S Bach.

A ______________ is used to join words that are to be read together, e.g. well-lit.

A ______________ car uses both a petrol engine and an electric motor.

3 Write the adjectives on these syllable slides.

sym	hy	sym	hyp	sys	sym
phon	gien	bol	not	tem	pa
ic	ic	ic	ic	at	thet
				ic	ic

WORD EXTRA liquid squalid

TARGETING SPELLING 6 © PASCAL PRESS ISBN 9781925490244

Don't confuse **symphony** and **sympathy**.
A **symphony** is a musical composition (from ***phono*** = *sound*).
Sympathy is a feeling of sadness shared with someone (from ***pathos*** = *feeling*).

4 Place a letter in each box to spell the missing words.

Water is made up of oxygen and _____.

Billy tea and damper with _____ is an old Aussie favourite.

A sore throat is a _____ of a cold.

The fireman connected the hose to a _____ in the street.

The dove is a _____ of peace.

The doctor gave me an injection with a hypodermic _____.

h	y						
s	y						
s	y						
h	y						
s	y						
s	y						

5 Can you say what these symbols mean?

6 A synopsis is a summary of a story or film. Write a synopsis of a story you have read recently, or a well-known folk tale.

Title ______________________

Synopsis

____

7 Unscramble these games played with a ball. Start with the letter in bold.

bea**b**slla ______ ko**h**yec ______ ni**t**nse ______

bkaetlalbs ______ quhas**s** ______ ikcr**c**te ______

Prefixes: ab-, ac-

The **prefix ab-** means 'from' or 'away', so ***abduct*** = *to lead away* (from ***duco ductus*** = *I lead*).
The **prefix ac-** means 'to' or 'with', so ***accurate*** = *done with care* (from ***curo*** = *I care*) and ***accelerate*** = *to hasten to* (from ***celer*** = *swift*).

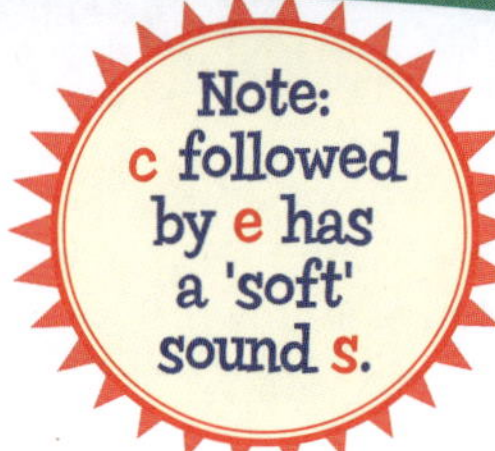

SEE & SAY

abduct	absent	abrupt	accept	account	accompany
absurd	absolute	abundant	access	accurate	accommodate
absorb	abdomen	abbreviate	accelerate	accomplish	accumulate

1 Add endings to the words in bold to complete the sentences.

absent John looked ____________________ out the train window at the passing scenery.

account Eyewitnesses gave several different ____________________ of the accident.

accelerate The racing car driver ____________________ down the final straight.

accomplish Cole was awarded a gold medal, ____________________ a lifetime dream.

accept Henry stepped forward and ____________________ the trophy for the team.

2 Colour the pairs of words that are synonyms. Use a different colour for each pair.

accurate	abduct	absurd	accomplish	abrupt	abundant	abbreviate
kidnap	plentiful	achieve	sudden	shorten	correct	silly

Don't confuse **accept** and **except**.
Accept means to happily receive something.
*Example: I will **accept** her party invitation.*
Except means leaving out or excluding someone/something.
*Example: Everyone is going to the game **except** me.*

WORD TRAPS

3 Add -ly to build adverbs and -ion to build nouns. *(Apply any rules and tips.)*

Add -ly		Add -ion	
accurate		abduct	
absolute		access	
abrupt		abbreviate	
abundant		accelerate	
absent		accumulate	
accidental		accommodate	

WORD EXTRA accident accrue

TARGETING SPELLING 6 © PASCAL PRESS ISBN 9781925490244

UNIT 24

4 Add the missing letters to mend the broken words.

I **acc** __ __ **t** __ __ an invitation to my cousin's birthday party.

We booked **acc** __ __ **m** __ **da** __ __ __ __ at a motel for one night.

Jinny is **ab** __ __ **n** __ from school because she is ill.

I used **ab** __ __ **rb** __ **n** __ paper to mop up the milk I spilled.

The car came to an **abr** __ __ **t** stop when the lights changed suddenly.

WORD TRAPS

Don't confuse **accomplish** (verb) and **accomplice** (noun).
If you **accomplish** a task, you complete it successfully.
An **accomplice** is a person who helps someone commit a crime.

5 Write one or two sentences about your greatest accomplishment.

____

____

____

6 *What do jelly babies wear on their feet?*
To find out, colour the box in front of the correct word to spell out the answer.

A sponge will ____ water very easily.	g	absorb	s	absurd
I read an interesting ____ of the diver's life.	l	discount	u	account
To win, you must ____ this task in ten minutes.	i	accompany	m	accomplish
Damage from the quake was widespread and ____.	b	absolute	p	obsolete
I hope the teacher will ____ my excuse for being late.	o	accept	p	access
For the best result, measurements must be ____.	e	accumulate	o	accurate
The ____ occurred at the corner of my street.	t	accident	r	accelerate
Deep in the forest, the path came to an ____ end.	s	abrupt	y	abduct

__ __ __ __ __ __ __ __

7 Match the words to their meanings.

ab scond	to make something stand out; highlight; underline
ab seil ing	to run away secretly to avoid being caught
ab sent ee	a person whose job is to examine the financial records of a business
ac count ant	sport of lowering oneself down a cliff using ropes
ac cuse	a person who is not present; who does not 'show up'
ac cent u ate	to blame someone for some wrongdoing

How many words can you remember?

Go back and choose any *See and Say* list. Read through it twice, focusing on how the words look and sound. Write as many words as you can remember in your notebook. Check how many you have written correctly and enter your score here. ☐

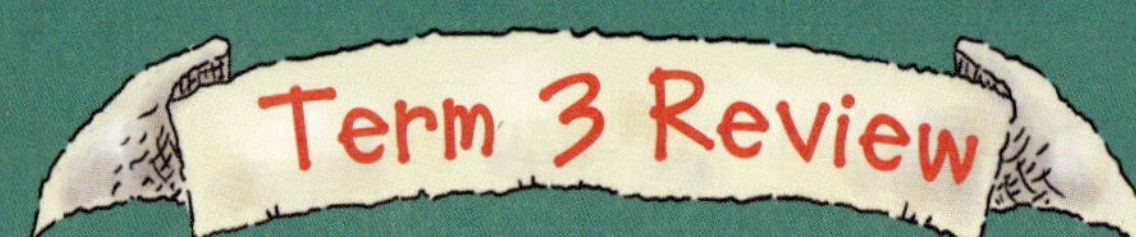

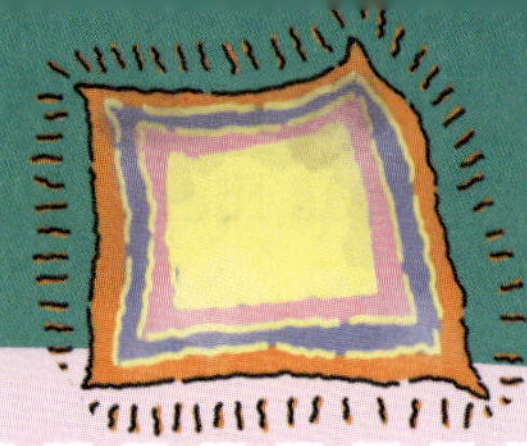

1 Name the pictures.

2 Write these nouns in plural form.

success ____________ remedy ____________ emotion ____________

industry ____________ decision ____________ account ____________

symptom ____________ process ____________ canary ____________

mystery ____________ symphony ____________ fallacy ____________

3 Complete this table of present and past tense verbs.

	Add -s or -es	Add -ing	Add -ed
process			
regulate			
absorb			
reduce			
propel			
accompany			
prohibit			
reminisce			

4 Write sentences to show the difference in meaning between: 1. precede and proceed, 2. access and excess, 3. accept and except.

1 ____

____

____

2 ____

____

____

3 ____

____

____

TARGETING SPELLING 6 © PASCAL PRESS ISBN 9781925490244

5 The suffixes -er and -or show 'one who' or 'that which' does something, e.g. *one who dances* is a *dancer*; *that which grates* is a *grater*. Choose the correct one to say who or what these people or things are.

One who or that which …

educates	____________	provides	____________
decorates	____________	propels	____________
produces	____________	processes	____________
refrigerates	____________	renovates	____________
regulates	____________	instructs	____________
conducts	____________	protects	____________

6 Use the meaning clues to mend the broken words.

correct	acc __ __ __ t __	kidnap	ab __ __ __ t
not present	a __ s __ __ t	look like	res __ __ b __ __
normal	or __ __ n __ __ y	speed up	ac __ __ l __ __ a __ __
wild	f __ r __ __	cure	r __ m __ d __
song for baby	l __ ll __ __ __	long trip	j __ __ __ n __ y
sign	sym __ __ __	on time	p __ __ __ t __ __ l

7 Add suffixes to build nouns. Choose from -ion (-tion, -sion), -ment or -ance.

entertain	____________	reduce	____________
endure	____________	conclude	____________
recommend	____________	enchant	____________
collide	____________	accept	____________
entitle	____________	precise	____________
resemble	____________	accompany	____________

8 Write a one-word answer to these questions.

What type of boat takes passengers across a river?	f____________
What are people who train at a gym?	g____________
What African dog-like animal scavenges for food?	h____________
What name is given to contaminated water, air and soil?	p____________
Mr is an _____ of mister.	ab____________
What is a room filled with books for reading/borrowing?	l____________
Water is comprised of oxygen and what other element?	h____________
Who keeps the beat for choirs and orchestras?	c____________
What is the largest segment of an ant's body?	ab____________
What are the following: water, milk, lemonade, petrol?	l____________

Suffixes: -ous, -ious

The **suffix** -ous (-ious and -eous) means 'full of', 'having' or 'being', so *prosperous = having prosperity*; *furious = full of fury*; *courteous = being considerate*.

SEE & SAY

curious	obvious	precious	courteous	porous	arduous
furious	various	spacious	gorgeous	pompous	enormous
devious	delicious	gracious	glamorous	prosperous	ravenous

1 Choose an adjective of similar meaning from the *See and Say* list for each of the following words.

angry **f**__________ beautiful **g**__________ valuable **p**__________

tasty **d**__________ huge **e**__________ roomy **s**__________

polite **c**__________ wealthy **p**__________ hungry **r**__________

2 Colour the pairs of words that are synonyms. Use a different colour for each pair.

arduous	obvious	various	pompous	devious	curious	gracious
inquisitive	haughty	dishonest	polite	difficult	assorted	clear

3 Add -ly to these adjectives to form adverbs of manner.

curious __________ generous __________

gracious __________ obvious __________

dangerous __________ enormous __________

furious __________ delicious __________

pompous __________ serious __________

4 Write the base word of each adjective, *e.g. famous, fame.*

furious __________ glamorous __________

gracious __________ spacious __________

dangerous __________ prosperous __________

disastrous __________ glorious __________

WORD EXTRA dangerous generous

TARGETING SPELLING 6 © PASCAL PRESS ISBN 9781925490244

UNIT 25

5 **Choose a suitable adjective from the *See and Say* list to describe each of these nouns.**

______	food	______	jewels
______	task	______	gentleman
______	elephant	______	children

6 **Add suffixes to form adjectives. Choose from -ous and -ful.**

joy	______	fame	______
adventure	______	hazard	______
plenty	______	fear	______
colour	______	doubt	______
courage	______	envy	______
mischief	______	victory	______

7 **Match each adjective to its noun form.**

curious	prosperity	various	generosity
prosperous	curio	gracious	enormity
anxious	courtesy	studious	variety
courteous	delicacy	generous	graciousness
delicious	anxiety	enormous	study

8 **Circle the spelling mistakes. Write them correctly in the box.**

Over four hundred years ago, a German astronomer named Johann Kepler exclaimed, "We must buld a ship to sail the oceans of space in the universe!" This became a realty in the 20th century with the landing of man on the moon and the lunching of many space probes to unraval the secrets of the stars. Using the powerfull Kepler telescope, NASA continues to probe the sky for signs of life on distant plants. In July 2016, an internashnal team of scientists announsed that they had discovered a four-planet solar system, 181 lightyears away, which may support life.

9 **Use the letters in this word to make new words. Write these words in columns in your notebook. Score your words and write your total score in the box.**

adventurous

Score 3 points for each 4-letter word.
Score 5 points for each 5-letter word.
Score 10 points for each 5+-letter word.

UNIT 26

Prefixes: dia- and Suffixes: -ile

dia- is a Greek **prefix** meaning 'through'. A ***diameter*** is *a line through the centre of a circle*.

-ile is a **suffix** showing 'capability' from the Latin ***ilis***, so *mobile* = *capable of moving* (from the Latin ***moveo motus*** = *I move*).

SEE & SAY

dial	diagnose	diameter	fertile	docile	sterile
dialect	diagram	diaphragm	futile	hostile	crocodile
dialogue	diagonal	diamond	agile	mobile	juvenile

Choose a word from the *See and Say* list to complete these sentences.

The hands of a clock move around the ____________________ to show time.

The saltwater ____________________ is large and aggressive with razor-sharp teeth.

Part of a doctor's job is to ____________________ and treat health problems.

The ____________________ is the hardest and most precious of all gemstones.

Sharna keeps in contact with her friends on her ____________________ phone.

The ____________________ of a circle is its width at the widest point.

Colour the pairs of words that are synonyms. Use a different colour for each pair.

dialogue	agile	futile	juvenile	diagram	docile	hostile
useless	unfriendly	gentle	drawing	talk	nimble	teenager

Change these adjectives to nouns by adding the suffix -ity, e.g. *fragile, fragility*.

fertile ____________________ agile ____________________

futile ____________________ docile ____________________

hostile ____________________ mobile ____________________

sterile ____________________ versatile ____________________

WORD TRAPS

Don't confuse **diary** and **dairy**.
A **diary** is a book for recording daily events.
A **dairy** is a place on a farm where cows are milked.
Dairy products include milk, cream, butter, cheese and yoghurt.

WORD EXTRA diary profile

TARGETING SPELLING 6 © PASCAL PRESS ISBN 9781925490244

UNIT 26

4 **Follow the arrows to write the verbs and nouns.** ***(Remember to drop the e.)***

fertile → ise → er / ation; **fertile** → ity

sterile → ise → er / ation; **sterile** → ity

mobile → ise → ation; **mobile** → ity

________	________	
________	________	________
________	________	________
________	________	________

Diagnosis is the noun formed from *diagnose*. Its plural form is ***diagnoses***. Its adjective form is ***diagnostic***.

5 **Add endings to the words in bold to complete the sentences.** ***(Apply any rules and tips.)***

diagnose After ________ the problem, the doctor prescribed medication.

diagonal Draw a line ________ from corner to corner.

diamond Coloured ________ are the most valuable of all.

docile The sheep walked ________ into the holding yard.

crocodile ________ are large, lizard-like reptiles living in tropical waters.

6 **Do some research and write a paragraph about crocodiles.**

____

____

____

____

____

____

7 **Add vowels to mend the broken words. Use the clues to help you.**
(Hint: All vowels in a word are different.)

M ___ ST ___ K ___	error
C ___ MM ___ N ___ C ___ T ___	to make contact with other people
___ BD ___ M ___ N	stomach; tummy
R ___ D ___ ___ S	a line from the centre to the edge of a circle
___ GN ___ R ___	shun; disregard
C ___ M ___ D ___ ___ N	a funny person
G ___ DG ___ TS	mechanical devices
___ NTHR ___ LL ___ NG	spellbinding; engrossing
CHR ___ N ___ CL ___	a record of events
T ___ L ___ PS	flowers famous in Holland

Suffixes: -able, -ible

-able and **-ible** are **adjective-forming suffixes** meaning 'able'.
*Examples: port**able*** means 'able to be carried'; *ed**ible*** means 'able to be eaten'.
As a general guide, **-able** is added to 'complete' words (e.g. *read**able**, break**able**, bear**able***), while **-ible** follows incomplete words of Latin origin.
*Examples: **video (visus)** = I see,* so *vis**ible*** means 'able to be seen'; ***audio** = I hear,* so *aud**ible*** means 'able to be heard'.

SEE & SAY

collectable	fashionable	hospitable	invisible	intelligible	combustible
durable	reasonable	tolerable	invincible	legible	admissible
desirable	valuable	manageable	infallible	audible	plausible

1 Choose an adjective from the *See and Say* list to match these meanings.

able to be read easily **l**________________
never being wrong **in**________________
able to be heard **a**________________
able to be understood **in**________________
able to be controlled **m**________________
unable to be seen **in**________________
easily set on fire **c**________________
unable to be defeated **in**________________

2 Colour the pairs of words that are synonyms. Use a different colour for each pair.

durable	plausible	valuable	hospitable	fashionable	admissible	tolerable
precious	stylish	friendly	bearable	believable	lasting	acceptable

When **adjectives** end in **-able** or **-ible**, change **le** to **il**, then add **-ity** to form **nouns**. *Examples: portable, portability; possible, possibility*

3 Using the tip above, build nouns from these adjectives.

durable ________________
probable ________________
infallible ________________
legible ________________
responsible ________________
invisible ________________
capable ________________
flexible ________________
reliable ________________
respectable ________________

WORD EXTRA probable possible

TARGETING SPELLING 6 © PASCAL PRESS ISBN 9781925490244

-able
There are thousands of words ending in **-able** and the number is growing as we add new words to our language. Recent ones include *rewrite**able*** (DVDs) and *blogg**able*** (material).

-ible
There are only about 180 words ending in **-ible**. No new words have been added for a very long time.

4 Colour the correct suffix. Choose from -able and -ible.

After ten years with the company, Mr Free is **elig** able/ible for long-service leave.

The school is **access** able/ible through a main gate and two side gates.

The men were found floating at sea in an **inflate** able/ible life raft.

The task is easily **achieve** able/ible in half an hour.

After **consider** able/ible thought, I have decided to paint my bike black.

Don't confuse **hospitable** and **hospital**.
A **hospitable** person is kind and generous to his or her guests.
A **hospital** is a place where sick and injured people receive medical treatment.

5 Add a prefix to write antonyms. Choose from in-, im- or un-.

_____desirable	_____reasonable	_____tolerable
_____inhabitable	_____possible	_____manageable
_____probable	_____visible	_____intelligible
_____audible	_____plausible	_____hospitable

Don't confuse **valuable**, **invaluable** and **valueless**.
Valuable means that something is worth a lot of money.
Invaluable means that something is so precious it is beyond price.
Valueless means that something is of no value at all.

6 Add the missing letters to mend the broken words.

I don't have a **pl** __ __ **s** __ __ **le** excuse for being late this morning.

You must write neatly and **l** __ **g** __ __ **l** __ so that I can read your work.

There are millions of stars that are **inv** __ **s** __ __ **l** __ to the naked eye.

Her cries for help were barely **a** __ **d** __ **b** __ __ above the wind and driving rain.

A warm and **h** __ __ **p** __ **t** __ __ **le** welcome awaited me when I entered the room.

Word Endings: -ure, -ude

Words ending in **-ure** and **-ude** come from Latin roots.
*Examples: end**ure** = to last or to bear* (from **durus** = *hard);*
*concl**ude** = to bring to a close* (from ***claudo clausus*** = *to close*)

SEE & SAY

posture	endure	assure	exude	prelude	attitude
pasture	mature	obscure	intrude	altitude	gratitude
pressure	demure	temperature	conclude	aptitude	fortitude

1 Add endings to the words in bold to complete the sentences.

exude ____________________ confidence, Andy strutted onto the tennis court.

demure Cassie smiled ____________________ and bowed her head.

conclude Jai played his final game, ____________________ a fine career in football.

assure The coach ____________________ his team they were well trained and ready to win.

obscure Fog rolled in, ____________________ our view across the valley.

2 Colour the pairs of words that are synonyms. Use a different colour for each pair.

conclude	pasture	altitude	obscure	aptitude	mature	fortitude
height	ability	ripe	grass	strength	end	hide/vague

3 Complete this table of present and past participles.

	Add -ing	Add -ed
assure		
obscure		
endure		
exude		
intrude		

4 Write a sentence about each of these words: temperature and gratitude.

____

____

____

____

WORD EXTRA

exclude sure

TARGETING SPELLING 6 © PASCAL PRESS ISBN 9781925490244

5 Build nouns by adding suffixes. Choose from -ion, -ity or -ance. *(Apply any rules or tips.)*

assure	______	intrude	______
conclude	______	obscure	______
mature	______	endure	______
invade	______	protrude	______
exclude	______	secure	______

6 Colour the correct word in the brackets.

Good [pasture posture] is an important aspect of dance.

I can [insure assure] you that you look as pretty as a picture.

It is impolite to [intrude conclude] on our conversation.

Due to injury, Mark will be [exuded excluded] from the match on Saturday.

Jeremy has a great [aptitude altitude] for maths and science.

7 Match these words to their meanings. Use a dictionary to help you.

lat it ude	a short period of time or rest; interval; recess
long it ude	the distance north or south of the equator measured in degrees
temp er a ment al	the size or extent of something; greatness; importance
in ter lude	a book/pamphlet containing information about a product/service
sig na ture	a picture exaggerating certain features to create a comic effect
brōch ure	someone moody, excitable, unpredictable, hot-headed
mag nit ude	the distance east or west of *Greenwich** measured in degrees
căr ic a ture	the growing of plants for their fruit, vegetables and flowers
hort i cult ure	name written in a distinctive way as a form of ID

* *Greenwich is in England.*

8 Write a letter in each box to spell the missing words in these sentences.

The ___ dropped below freezing point overnight.

He gave me a bunch of flowers to express his ___.

She applied ___ to the wound to stop the bleeding.

Leo has a great ___ to his work and always tries his best.

Sheep are grazing in the green ___.

Mount Everest has an ___ of 8848 m above sea level.

t										
g	r									
p	r									
a	t									
p										
a	l									

How many words can you remember?

Go back and choose any *See and Say* list. Read through it twice, focusing on how the words look and sound. Write as many words as you can remember in your notebook. Check how many you have written correctly and enter your score here. ☐

Letter Teams: qu, ph

qu is written together as one unit of sound. This sound was originally written as **kw**, but was replaced by **qu** about 700 years ago. It is usually pronounced as **kw** (*queen, quick, quiet*), but there are some words where it is pronounced as **k** (*bouquet, conquer, mosque*).

Words containing **ph** are of Greek origin.
Examples: graph (from ***grapho*** *= I write*), ***physics*** (*from* ***physica*** *= natural things*), ***pharmacy*** (from ***pharmacon*** *= a remedy*)

SEE & SAY

bouquet	mosque	conquer	dolphin	pharmacy	sapphire
banquet	mosquito	tranquil	graph	phenomenal	orphan
antique	physique	sequence	phoney	pharaoh	typhoon

Choose a word from the *See and Say* list to complete these sentences.

A ____________________ is a slender biting insect that breeds in stagnant water.

A ____________________ is a building where Muslims go to worship.

A ____________________ is a transparent, precious gemstone, typically blue in colour.

A ____________________ is stocked with a wide range of products to benefit our health.

The opera singer was presented with a large ____________________ of flowers.

2 Write these nouns in plural form.

typhoon	mosquito	orphan	graph
__________	__________	__________	__________
sapphire	dolphin	sequence	banquet
__________	__________	__________	__________

Colour the pairs of words that are synonyms. Use a different colour for each pair.

typhoon	antique	pharaoh	tranquil	phoney	conquer	banquet
feast	defeat	hurricane	fake	calm	ancient	king

Be a word builder. *(Apply any rules and tips.)*

* Remember to double l.

orphan + age	__________	pharmacy + ist	__________
conquer + or	__________	tranquil + ity *	__________
bio + graph + y	__________	tranquil + ise *	__________
antique + ity	__________	graph + ic	__________

WORD EXTRA equator elephant

TARGETING SPELLING 6 © PASCAL PRESS ISBN 9781925490244

Don't confuse **physics** and **physique**.
Physics is the study of matter and energy.
Your **physique** is the shape of your body.

5 Read down the syllable slides. Match the number of each word to its meaning.

1	2	3	4	5	6
con sē quence	phen om en on	pho tō graph	quin tup lets	ē quest ri an	em pha sis

- ☐ five babies born at the same time
- ☐ unusual occurrence not always understood
- ☐ horse rider (noun); relating to horseriding (adj)
- ☐ image taken by a camera
- ☐ result of an action, usually unpleasant
- ☐ stress/importance placed on something

6 Circle the spelling mistakes. Write them correctly in the box.

The great steed snorted and poured the ground, held in check by its rider Sir Ralph de Berg, a brave and intrepud knight. The iron gate rattled upward, and horse and rider burst across the lowerd drawbridge at break-neck speed. Sir Ralph had been dispatched on a desprate quest to rescue the Lady Catherine, who had been kidnapt by enemies of the king during a daring night raid.

By nightfall, he had reached the outskirts of the enemy's camp and drew in the horse's rains. He tethered his trusty steed to a tree and crept soundlessly forward towards the gathring of tents. He caught a glimpse of the Lady Catherine, arms tied, as she was pushed ruffly into a tent at the edge of the camp. Sir Ralph drew back into the shadows and circled his way around the camp until he was behind the Lady's tent …

7 How does the story end? It is yours to complete.

Suffixes: -ian, -ial

-ian is a **noun-forming suffix** signifying a *person*, e.g. one who plays music is a *musician*; one who makes eyeglasses is an *optician*.
-ial is an **adjective-forming suffix** meaning 'of' or 'belonging to', e.g. *social = belonging to society*; *spatial = of space*. Words ending in **-ial** can also be **nouns**, e.g. *sports official, TV commercial, weekly special*

SEE & SAY

musician	optician	guardian	martial	initial	special
technician	politician	comedian	partial	essential	crucial
electrician	beautician	pedestrian	official	spatial	commercial

1 Choose a word from the *See and Say* list to complete these sentences. Add endings where necessary.

In cities, people use a ____________________ crossing to safely cross main streets.

Federal ____________________ meet in parliament to make laws to govern our country.

You will see many advertisements on ____________________ television.

I bought a new pair of glasses from an ____________________.

An orchestra is made up of many ____________________ playing a range of instruments.

2 Colour the pairs of words that are synonyms. Use a different colour for each pair.

partial	initial	crucial	official	pedestrian	special	guardian
walker	formal	partly	beginning	extraordinary	protector	important

An **optometrist** tests eyesight and prescribes corrective lenses.
An **optician** makes the eyeglasses with the prescribed lenses.
You would buy eyeglasses at an **optical** store.

3 Build adverbs of manner by adding **-ly**. *Example: beneficial, beneficially*

official	____________________	essential	____________________
partial	____________________	spatial	____________________
initial	____________________	special	____________________
crucial	____________________	commercial	____________________
social	____________________	racial	____________________

WORD EXTRA social racial

TARGETING SPELLING 6 © PASCAL PRESS ISBN 9781925490244

UNIT 30

4 Replace **-ian** with **-al** to change these nouns to adjectives.

musician	musical	optician	______
technician	______	politician	______
electrician	______	mathematician	______
magician	______	clinician	______

5 The suffixes **-ian**, **-ist**, **-er** and **-or** are added to name people (or things) that have certain jobs, e.g. *a person who dances is a dancer*. Add a suffix to name these people.

One who…

performs alone	**s**______	plays music	**m**______
installs electric wiring	**e**______	plays a piano	**p**______
treats sick people	**d**______	jogs to keep fit	**j**______
makes people laugh	**c**______	leads an orchestra	**c**______
draws cartoons	**c**______	carves statues	**s**______

6 Write the nouns from which these adjectives have been built.

beneficial	benefit	bacterial	______
financial	______	facial	______
equatorial	______	pictorial	______
colonial	______	memorial	______

7 The world is full of magical things. Who knows what one may find in rainbows and shadows, and beneath clouds and moonlight? Write an imaginative story about a magic stone and a black cat.

Suffixes: -ent, -ant

When the Latin **suffixes -ent** and **-ant** are added to words, they form mostly **nouns** and **adjectives**. Because these suffixes are unstressed, they have a 'schwa' sound **(uh)**. For this reason, you will need to pay attention to what words *look* like. Many nouns ending in **-ant** signify *people*.
*Examples: assist**ant**, attend**ant**, serv**ant***

SEE & SAY

dependent	efficient	evident	assistant	dependant	consonant
despondent	different	obedient	attendant	defendant	confidant
confident	insolent	magnificent	servant	dominant	relevant

Choose a word from the *See and Say* list to complete these sentences. Add endings where necessary.

Lee's dog is very ____________________ and will sit on command.

The street parade was a lively and ____________________ spectacle.

The ____________________ stood in the courthouse dock accused of car theft.

There are many ____________________ varieties of fruit to choose from.

Wealthy people often hire ____________________ to maintain their households.

Colour the pairs of words that are synonyms. Use a different colour for each pair.

evident	assistant	confident	despondent	different	efficient	insolent
sad	competent	rude	self-assured	obvious	unalike	helper

Don't confuse **dependent** (adjective) and **dependant** (noun).
A **dependent** person relies on someone for support.
*Example: Mr and Mrs Jones have three **dependent** children.*
Someone in need of support is called a **dependant**.
*Example: Mr Ellis is a single man with no **dependants**.*

Add -ly to form adverbs of manner.

independent	____________________	confident	____________________
obedient	____________________	magnificent	____________________
evident	____________________	despondent	____________________
insolent	____________________	efficient	____________________
frequent	____________________	pleasant	____________________

WORD EXTRA

recent decent

TARGETING SPELLING 6 © PASCAL PRESS ISBN 9781925490244

Add vowels to mend the broken words.

There are fifty **c __ nt __ st __ nts** in the beauty **p __ ge __ nt.**

Jake is in trouble for being **dis __ b __ d __ ent** and **ins __ l __ nt.**

There is one major **s __ ttl __ m __ nt** on the island with 1000 **inh __ b __ t __ nts.**

Sally has become a **c __ nf __ d __ nt** and **eff __ ci __ nt** speller.

Eyewitnesses gave **d __ ff __ r __ nt** accounts of the car **acc __ d __ nt.**

The words in the English **l __ ng __ __ g __** are comprised of vowels and **c __ ns __ n __ nts.**

The suffixes -ent and -ant are replaced by -ence/-ency and -ance/-ancy to form nouns. Complete this table.

-ent → -ence	-ant → -ance	-ent → -ency	-ant → -ancy
confident confidence	assistant	despondent	infant
evident	attendant	dependent	consultant
obedient	dominant	efficient	expectant
magnificent	relevant	competent	accountant
insolent	brilliant	frequent	hesitant
dependent	important	decent	vacant

Don't confuse **confident** and **confidant**.
A **confident** person is sure of themselves and certain about things.
*Example: I am **confident** I can pass the spelling test.*
A **confidant** is someone you can trust with your secrets.
*Examples: My big brother is my best friend and **confidant**.*

Add vowels to mend the broken words. Use the clues to help you. *(Hint: All vowels in a word are different.)*

P __ SS __ SS __ NG	having or owning
W __ DDL __ D	moved like a duck
T __ __ ST __ R	a device used at breakfast time
__ BST __ CL __	a hurdle or barrier
M __ N __ M __ NT	a statue erected in memory of a person
__ MP __ ST __ R	a phoney; person pretending to be someone else
M __ M __ NT __ RY	lasting a very short time; fleeting
P __ NC __ RS	the front claws of a crab or lobster
C __ RC __ S	a travelling show
__ RD __ N __ RY	plain; normal; not outstanding

Suffixes: -ence, -ance

-ence and -ance are **noun-forming suffixes**. Derived from Latin, they signify a *state, action* or *quality*. *Examples: reli**ance** = state of relying on someone/thing; def**ence** = an action of defending*
Because these **suffixes** are unstressed, they have a 'schwa' sound **(uh)**. For this reason, you will need to pay attention to what words *look* like.

SEE & SAY

defence	impudence	occurrence	balance	radiance	extravagance
influence	conference	prominence	ambulance	reliance	compliance
incidence	reference	experience	appliance	elegance	maintenance

1 Circle any words in the brackets that are similar in meaning to the words in bold.

An **elegant** person is [slender stylish lonely fashionable].
A **prominent** person is [predictable plump famous renowned].
A **compliant** person is [obedient smug dutiful fault-finding].
An **extravagant** person is [common wasteful flamboyant reckless].
An **impudent** person is [rude foolish noisy cheeky].
A **magnificent** person is [large magnetic marvellous wonderful].

2 Colour the pairs of words that are synonyms. Use a different colour for each pair.

defence	maintenance	influence	balance	occurrence	reference	radiance
upkeep	steadiness	happening	glow	protection	effect	mention

3 Write the base verbs. Then write the present and past participles.

defence	defend	defending	defended
occurrence			
reliance			
conference			
maintenance			
reference			

Don't confuse incidents and incidence.
Incidents are happenings or events.
*Example: My friend recounted several amusing **incidents** from his recent trip.*
Incidence refers to the rate or frequency of something happening.
*Example: There has been a sharp increase in the **incidence** of the Zika virus.*

WORD EXTRA fence chance

TARGETING SPELLING 6 © PASCAL PRESS ISBN 9781925490244

UNIT 32

4 Add noun suffixes to words you have been learning throughout the year. *(Apply any rules and tips.)*

Add -ance		Add -ence	
assure		depend	
endure		obedient	
observe		interfere	
guide		transfer	
perform		reminisce	
admit		emerge	
resemble		precede	

5 Use different suffixes to write new words. *(Apply any rules and tips.)*

rely < ant ______ / ance ______

defy < ant ______ / ance ______

comply < ant ______ / ance ______

refer < ee ______ / ence ______

exist < ent ______ / ence ______

excel < ent ______ / ence ______

ignore < ant ______ / ance ______

persist < ent ______ / ence ______

depend < ent ______ / ence ______

import < ant ______ / ance ______

6 Match these words to their meanings. Use a dictionary to help you.

ig nor ance → (a lack of knowledge)	the ability to accept opinions and beliefs that are different to your own
rĕf er end um	a lack of knowledge
vĭg ĭl ance	things happening together by chance
tol er ance	failure to take proper care and attention
cō in cĭd ence	a state of being alert and watchful
al lī ance	a public (yes/no) vote on a question of government or law
nĕg li gence	an agreement to work together to achieve a result

How many words can you remember?

Go back and choose any *See and Say* list. Read through it twice, focusing on how the words look and sound. Write as many words as you can remember in your notebook. Check how many you have written correctly and enter your score here. ☐

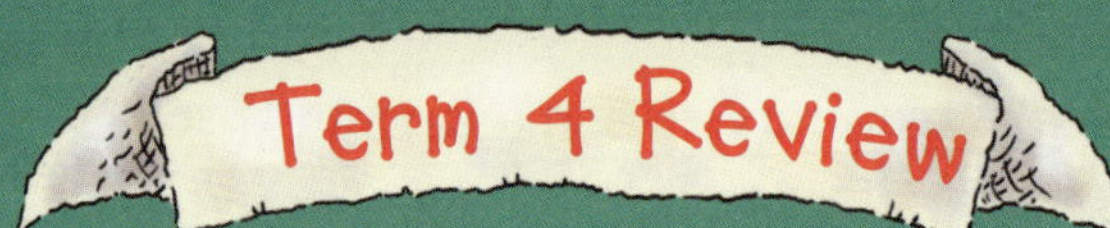

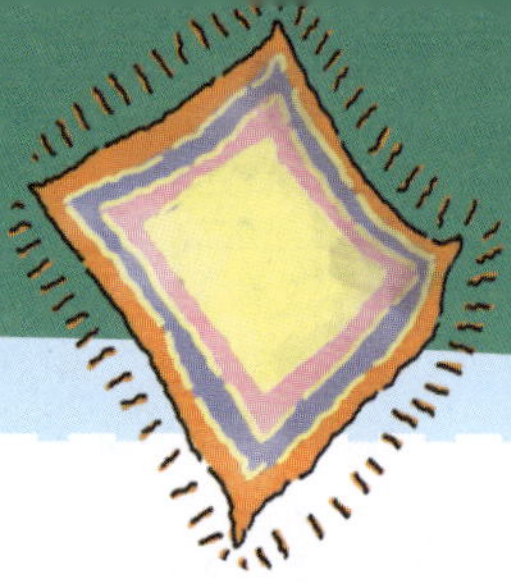

1 **Name the pictures.**

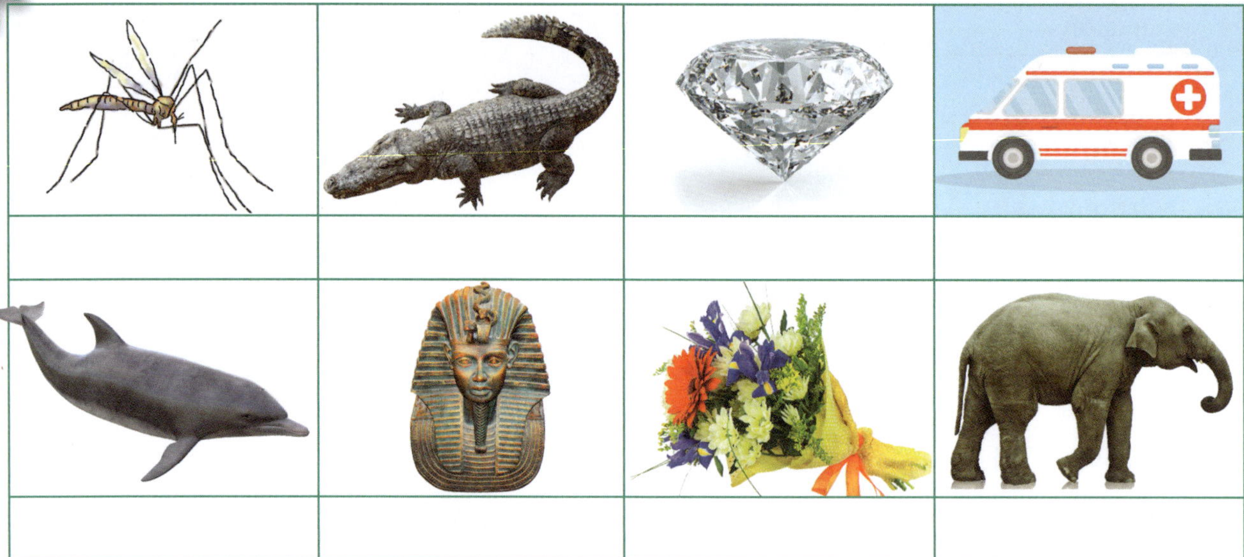

Complete this table of present and past tense verbs.

	Add -s or -es	Add -ing	Add -ed
endure			
rely			
conclude			
occur			
excel			

Colour the correct word in the brackets.

Rupert is [confidant confident] he will pass his music exam.

The accident victims were taken to [hospitable hospital] by ambulance.

We must [exclude exude] you from the team if you are unwell.

It is not yet [probable possible] to travel to Mars in a manned spaceship.

After many successful conquests, Napoleon felt [invisible invincible].

Use the meaning cues to mend the broken words.

helper	as _ _ _ t _ _ t	cheeky	im _ _ d _ _ t
defeat	c _ _ qu _ _	productive	f _ _ t _ l _
feast	b _ n _ _ _ t	clock face	d _ _ l
youth	j _ v _ n _ _ _	body shape	ph _ s _ _ _ _
inquisitive	c _ r _ _ _ s	technical drawing	dia _ _ _ _
advertisement	com _ _ r _ _ _ l	heat measure	t _ mp _ _ _ t _ _ _

TARGETING SPELLING 6 © PASCAL PRESS ISBN 9781925490244

5 Complete this word quiz. *(Hint: All answers end in -able or -ible.)*

What is an adjective that describes:

something able to be seen? v________________

something able to be heard? a________________

something long-lasting or hard-wearing? d________________

someone who is dressed in the latest style? f________________

handwriting that is easy to read? l________________

something that is precious or of great worth? v________________

material that could catch fire? c________________

someone who is friendly, warm and welcoming? h________________

6 Write antonyms by adding the prefixes in-, im- or un-.

_____fertile	_____desirable	_____efficient
_____possible	_____experienced	_____probable
_____confident	_____manageable	_____glamorous
_____tolerable	_____mature	_____reasonable

7 Add the suffixes -ion, -ian or -ity to build nouns.

collect	____________	special	____________
music	____________	conclude	____________
mature	____________	guard	____________
exclude	____________	hostile	____________
antique	____________	electric	____________

8 Write a word to match each meaning. *(Hint: All words end in -ent or -ant.)*

c________________ letters of the alphabet, excluding vowels

d________________ not the same

o________________ following orders; doing as you are told

d________________ relying on someone for support

s________________ person employed to maintain a household

c________________ self-assured; believing in oneself

f________________ happening very often

r________________ happening not long ago

9 Write sentences to show the difference in meaning between diary and dairy.

____

____

____

____

The Top 3 Spelling Rules

Rules	How to apply the rule	Examples
1 Doubling rule	When there is only ONE consonant after a short vowel, **double** that consonant before you add ***-ing*, *-ed*, *-y*, *-er*** or ***-est***.	hop hopping skip skipped fun funny big bigger biggest
	If there are already TWO consonants after the short vowel, just add an ending.	jump jumping pack packed dust dusty rich richer richest
2 The *e* rule	When a word ends in ***e***, drop the ***e*** before adding an ending that begins with a vowel or ***y***.	ride riding shine shiny gentle gently fame famous
	Do NOT drop the ***e*** when adding ***-ly*** (or any suffix beginning with a consonant).	safe safely safety use useful useless state statement
3 The *y* rule	When a noun ends in ***y***, follow these simple rules to write its plural: 1 If the letter before the ***y*** is a vowel, just add ***-s***. 2 If the letter before the ***y*** is NOT a vowel, change ***y*** to ***i*** and add ***-es***.	boys days monkeys baby babies lady ladies
	When a regular verb ends in ***y***, follow these simple rules to write it in present or past tense: 1 Just add ***-ing***. 2 If the letter before the ***y*** is a vowel, just add ***-s*** or ***-ed***. 3 If the letter before the ***y*** is NOT a vowel, change ***y*** to ***i*** and add ***-es*** or ***-ed***.	fly flying carry carrying play plays played enjoy enjoys enjoyed cry cries cried hurry hurries hurried
	When an adjective ends in ***y***, change ***y*** to ***i*** and add ***-er*** or ***-est*** (comparing) and ***-ly*** (adverbs of manner).	happier happiest happily lazier laziest lazily busy busier busiest busily

Common Endings

Ending	Purpose	Examples	Rule
-s	Add ***-s*** to MOST nouns to write them in plural form. Add ***-s*** to present tense verbs when the subject is *'he'*, *'she'* or *'it'*.	dogs apples toys hats runs plays rains growls eats stares swims	
-es	Add ***-es*** to nouns and verbs that end in **s**, **ss**, ***z***, ***zz***, ***x***, ***sh***, ***ch***.	buses dishes foxes tosses buzzes itches	
-ing	Add ***-ing*** to verbs to make present participles.	going jumping crying hopping rideing	1, 2, 3
-ed	Add ***-ed*** to *regular* verbs to make past participles.	planted clapped played carried baked	1, 2, 3
-y	Add ***-y*** to form adjectives.	bumpy funny stoney	1, 2
-er -est	Add ***-er*** or ***-est*** to show how adjectives and adverbs compare.	bigger biggest busier busiest faster fastest closer closest	1, 2, 3
-ly	Add ***-ly*** to form adverbs of manner.	quickly lately firstly noisily	2, 3

Suffixes

Noun						Adjective				Verb	
-age	courage	*-er*	dancer	*-ity*	hostility	*-able*	portable	*-ic*	basic	*-ate*	operate
-ant	servant	*-ent*	president	*-ion*	action	*-al*	local	*-ile*	mobile	*-en*	harden
-ance	reliance	*-ence*	experience	*-ment*	argument	*-ial*	special	*-ious*	precious	*-er*	flutter
-ar	beggar	*-hood*	childhood	*-ness*	darkness	*-en*	wooden	*-ish*	foolish	*-fy*	signify
-ary	dictionary	*-ian*	musician	*-or*	doctor	*-ent*	insolent	*-ive*	active	*-ise*	criticise
-ee	referee	*-ist*	pianist	*-ory*	directory	*-ful*	joyful	*-less*	careless		
-eer	pioneer	*-ism*	racism	*-ship*	friendship	*-ible*	visible	*-ous*	famous		

TARGETING SPELLING 6 © PASCAL PRESS ISBN 9781925490244